THIS IS ME I AM...

DREAMS AND AMBITIONS

Edited By Sarah Waterhouse

First published in Great Britain in 2024 by:

YoungWriters® Est. 1991

Young Writers
Remus House
Coltsfoot Drive
Peterborough
PE2 9BF
Telephone: 01733 890066
Website: www.youngwriters.co.uk

Printed and bound in the UK by BookPrintingUK
Website: www.bookprintinguk.com
YB0573BZ

AMBITIOUS
OPTIMISTIC
LONELY
CREATIVE
KIND
PROUD
ANGRY
SHY HAPPY
LOYAL ANXIOUS
PASSIONATE
CONFIDENT
STRONG
ADVENTUROUS
BRAVE BORED
FEARLESS
SENSITIVE
EXTROVERTED
INTROVERTED
SAD STRESSED
AFRAID
MISUNDERSTOOD
FRUSTRATED

FOREWORD

Since 1991, here at Young Writers we have celebrated the awesome power of creative writing, especially in young adults where it can serve as a vital method of expressing their emotions and views about the world around them. In every poem we see the effort and thought that each student published in this book has put into their work and by creating this anthology we hope to encourage them further with the ultimate goal of sparking a life-long love of writing.

Our latest competition for secondary school students, This Is Me: I Am..., challenged young writers to write about themselves, considering what makes them unique and expressing themselves freely and honestly, something which is so important for these young adults to feel confident and listened to. There were no restrictions on style or subject so you will find an anthology brimming with a variety of poetic styles and topics. We hope you find it as absorbing as we have.

We encourage young writers to express themselves and address subjects that matter to them, which sometimes means writing about sensitive or contentious topics. If you have been affected by any issues raised in this book, details on where to find help can be found at www.youngwriters.co.uk/info/other/contact-lines

CONTENTS

Sami Amin (12)	76
Shrey Mathur (15)	77
Yan Olsen (12)	78
Freya A (12)	79
Onyx Burden (14)	80
Michael Hill (14)	81
Abigail Flynn (14)	82
Kayley White (15)	83
Faizaan Khan (12)	84
Zaid Mohamed (12)	85
Jasmin Byrne (14)	86
Khanak Tiwari (12)	87
Ellie Thompson (15)	88
Olivia-Grace Weaver (12)	89
Abi Dodd (14)	90
Daniel Bowen (12)	91
Eleanor Shaw (12)	92
Alice Fu (14)	93
Aila Jaufferdeen (12)	94
Violet Mazanzi (14)	95
Theo Ranganathan (14)	96
Maqil Zawahir (12)	97
Ayaan Goraya (12)	98
Julian Szmulka	99

Hornchurch High School, Hornchurch

Grace Kingston (11)	100
Danny-Junior Kelly (13)	102
Eta Joshi (14)	103
Jack Bailey	104
Courtney Cross (12)	106
Joan Ukpokolo (12)	107
Ashmeet Kaur (12)	108
Teddy Thompson (11)	109
Jaeleen Ofosu (11)	110
Joyce Amusan (12)	111
Zipporah Gokhul (12)	112
Syed Shah (13)	113
Harvey Irish-Jones (12)	114
Alexander Kraster (13)	115
Isabelle Gjoni-Rakipaj (12)	116
Tomilola Hassan (11)	117

Matthew Boyes (11)	118
Perry Nkeng (11)	119
Parker-J Harper (11)	120
Roman Hartley (12)	121
Abdul Zahir Ali (11)	122
Auguste Guzauskaite (12)	123
Aamani Bains (11)	124
Kofi Crontsil (11)	125
Isabelle Kersey (12)	126
Alfie Champion (12)	127
Isabella Terrochaine (13)	128
Humayra Islam (12)	129
Amy Asowata (13)	130
Dennie Hardwicke (12)	131
Tarif Rehan (12)	132
Zane Thompson (11)	133
Amarah Duffy (11)	134
Jeremiah Quamina (12)	135
Nicholas Burghelea (11)	136
Maci Moore (11)	137
Zara Kasule (11)	138
Alice Mae Joy (11)	139
Jannat Kaur (13)	140
Sofiia Varvarych (11)	141
Jaimee Hardwicke (12)	142
Sadie Brewer (13)	143
Samuel Olaru (11)	144
Rahul Gunputh (11)	145
Anna Vimal (13)	146
Sienna Bird (11)	147
Musa Ahmed (12)	148
Lewis Hallel (12)	149
Amala Maria Baiju (12)	150
Dustin Ramirez-Vera (11)	151
Melissa Marshall (11)	152
Grace Gibbons (12)	153
Sephora Nsongo (12)	154
Dolcie Powell Bryan (13)	155
John Erdozo (11)	156
Kaitlin Ciobotaru (11)	157
Nandika Sharma (13)	158
Freddie Debruin (11)	159
Manikarnika Rai (13)	160

Alarmelu Aiswarya Periyakaruppan (12)   161
Niamh Spindler (12)   162
Matt Dixey (12)   163
Sururah Ilelaboye (11)   164
Bryan Aikpitanyi (12)   165
Lacey Butler (11)   166
Hollie-May Scott (13)   167
Rehnuma Tajrin (11)   168
Kaan Isikgun (11)   169
Archie Wyatt (13)   170
Naya Garcia Clegg (11)   171
Esi Amoa-Sakyi (13)   172
Daria-Gabriela Hululei (11)   173
Ibrahim Yusuf (12)   174
Ava Munday (11)   175
Juliette Jogaila (12)   176
Freddie Jones (13)   177
Nicole Nykante (12)   178
Izabela Pultinza (11)   179
Ronnie Holloway (11)   180
Kayla Cooper (11)   181
Mehek Bhuiyan (11)   182
Charlotte Miles (14)   183
Gracie Bennett (12)   184
Robert Dunas (11)   185
Chloe Butler (13)   186
Divine Apinoko (13)   187
Spencer Wheeler (11)   188
Alizah Islam (12)   189
Alex Buterchi (12)   190
Ryann Rookard (14)   191
Tyler Allen (14)   192

Hylands School, Chelmsford

John-James Read (11)   193
Persephonie Searson (12)   194
Ivy-Sola Gaci (11)   195
Albie Lodge (11)   196
Tommy-Alfie Read (12)   197

Millgate School, Leicester

Callum Wilson (13)   198
Finley Penfold (13)   200
Zaak Bate   201
Coby Newcomb (13)   202
Riegan Douglas (15)   203
Henry Ind (15)   204
Harvey Taylor Foster (13)   205
Raven Whitworth (13)   206
Declan Mark Kean (15)   207
Alex McCarthy (13)   208
Mason Russell (13)   209
Daisy Chapman (13)   210
Matilda Coley (13)   211
Liam Kirk (14)   212
Simon Ely (14)   213
Codey Wright-Prime (15)   214
Carson Birch (15)   215
Oliver Newitt (13)   216
Kaydon Jones (13)   217

Norton College, Norton

Elaine Nyashanu (13)   218
Emily Umpleby (13)   220
Lottie Johnson (13)   222
Albert Stokes (13)   224
Julia Piechowiak (13)   225
Kacie Marshall (13)   226
Cadence Joyce-Smith (11) & Naomi Tomasi   227
Jessica Thomas (12)   228
Molly Sterriker (12)   230
Erin Cotton (12)   231
Sylvie Hill (12)   232
Cadence Joyce-Smith (11)   233

DIFFERENT RELAXED FUN LONELY
STRONG FIERCE POSITIVE
OPTIMISTIC ADVENTUROUS
PASSIONATE HAPPY
ANXIOUS

THE POEMS

EXTROVERTED STRESSED
FEARLESS AMBITIOUS
LOYAL ANGRY
MISUNDERSTOOD OK PROUD
GRATEFUL FINE
TOUGH
STRONG BORED SAD INTROVERTED
WISE
CHILL ENERGETIC
UPBEAT BRAVE
KIND
WISE
QUIET TRUSTWORTHY

"This Is Me."

This is me, unique and true,
A spirit that's vibrant through and through,
With a passion so strong like a burning flame,
I hope I achieve and lead to fame,

From my dressage to my jumping,
I try to excel,
Oh, mightily I have a story to tell,
The thrill of riding, it feels so rare,
An equine passion beyond compare
This is my safety, my refugee, my home,
Where the feeling of warmth freely roams,

My friends and family, their hearts so kind,
But my nan, a treasure, forever in my mind
There, my refuge, a place to find peace,
Where my worries and troubles can finally cease,

This is me, my name's Florie Mae,
And my birthday is the 27th of May,
I live with my mum, dad and sister,
And all they do is the opposite of whisper,

But this is me, I know my safe place,
My home, my refuge, my life's very base.

Florie Mae Hymus (13)
Blackfen School For Girls, Sidcup

This Is Me

I am kind and loyal, a true good friend at heart.
I am disciplined and smart, you see, an academic
overachiever from the start.

Beyond the veil of perception lies a land of wonder. Often,
the magical path leads me to weave my own tapestries of
imagination, creating worlds of my own to help me escape
from reality.
To craft my own little world where I find peace and my spirit
soars free.

Beyond the treasures of kindred and good friends lies a
beautiful spell that enchants my heart:
art.
Art is about letting your mind and soul fly freely out of the
cage, like birds,
to create an enchanted piece of artwork.

The artist of life owns her power to create a dream life.
To her, life is an art - the ultimate embodiment of self-
expression. As her life unfolds, so does her masterpiece. One
stroke leads to another, and the painting comes to life.
Her very own little world.
The true beauty of art resides in *your* heart and soul.

Within the pages of literature lies an invitation to traverse
realms unknown,
to embark on voyages that kindle the flames of imagination.

Each word, a mystic, alluring piece, contributes to a grand
puzzle, unravelling
secrets and truths that transcend the fabric of reality. This
art,
this magic, holds a special place in my heart,
for it is a realm
where I am most skilled and my spirit takes flight to the
highest peak of inspiration.

Amidst the tempestuous seas of despair,
when the snares
of malevolence strive to devour me,
I seek
solace and refuge in the unwavering light, of my truest
friend and faith. The divine - the almighty
and all benevolent God.

My dear friend, you have but only glimpsed a fragment of
my essence from this poem.
Within me lies a boundless universe where stars and
galaxies twirl in cosmic dance.
Yet, amidst this grand expanse,
rests a kingdom of dreams and ambitions, a land of mystery
and magic, where secrets whisper in the wind, waiting to be
uncovered...

Thisaniyaa Ratnarasa (13)
Blackfen School For Girls, Sidcup

The Forest's Embrace

In the heart of the forest's warm embrace
A refuge found in nature's quiet grace
Amidst the trees, their branches intertwined
A sanctuary for the wandering mind

The forest stands as nature's steadfast wall
Where ancient secrets in its shadows fall
Each tree a guardian, their roots intertwined
A haven where the troubled soul can hide

Like leaves that flutter in the gentle breeze
In this refuge, worries find their ease
The forest whispers a soothing song
Where weary souls can mend what's wrong

In deepened sunlight, hope begins to grow,
As wildflowers in the greenery start to bestow
A refuge found within the emerald canopy
Where life's complexities untangle around me

The forest teaches lessons deep and wise
In its stillness, hidden truths arise
With energy buzzing through the fallen leaf,
A refuge for the dreamer, a tranquil dream.

So, seek the forest when the world is a storm
Where nature's refuge will transform
In its midst, you'll seek your spirit's key
A sanctuary beneath the green canopy.

Olivia Ferdinand-Brown (13)
Blackfen School For Girls, Sidcup

Where Oh Where Is My True Home?

Where oh where is my true home?
The streets of London are lively at this time
But no matter which way I search or roam
Someone to take me I cannot find

Someone who's kind and has compassion
Someone to take care of me.
Someone who has a good sense of fashion
To help get the clothes I need.

Where oh where is my true home?
Is it even in this city?
But no matter how far I search or roam
No one I find feels pity.

"To the countryside," I say to myself
To find a better home for me
I see a house in the distance and take a look
But no one I can see

Let's live here for a while, my consciousness said
And so my life begins
Twenty years go by and I haven't any sins

One day, as I was making some food
I heard a knock on the door

Suddenly, a bullet hit me
And I was lying on the floor.

I never got to see my mother
But I really wish I did.
There is one thing I'll always remember
'Home is where the heart is'.

Charlotte Underwood (12)
Blackfen School For Girls, Sidcup

What's The Rush?

Our human lives can be for over ninety years,
while my dog's will never reach beyond twenty.
As my mind gets intertwined,
leaving any mess and stress behind,
he's in the fields of flowers for hours;
chasing the bugs and the hues of gold from the sunset.

The need to fulfil the future burdens my brain,
not knowing what my story beholds,
though he's never had to turn a chapter as each of his
pages are the same.

Although there's no timer, time feels like it's ticking;
will I make ends meet and have shoes under my feet?
Or will the regret of not doing enough drag me by the
ankle?

His life is so small, yet so radiant,
and mine still feels unachieved.
The funny thing is, I'm only thirteen.
So, my question is,
what's the rush?

Mia Laville (13)
Blackfen School For Girls, Sidcup

Seeking Sanctuary

In a world overflowing with uncertainty and deprivation,
refugees embark on a life of isolation.
Amidst adversities, they strive with rectitude.
Their exodus a testament to fortitude.

A blood-curdling cry, I could hear them behind me.
Echoes of anticipation as we all tried to flee.
Cautious and apprehensive,
thoughts ran through my head, feeling pensive.

Danger crept closer: it was near,
I held my sister with meticulousness, shedding a tear.
I was uncertain about the course of action to take,
unsure of the diverse paths, one is a mistake.

An endeavour for solace, a journey marked,
promising that we would never be apart.
I witnessed my home shatter in a matter of seconds,
covering her eyes as he pulled out a weapon.

Kaylee Chu (13)
Blackfen School For Girls, Sidcup

This Is Me

This right here is me,
This right here is who I am.
Just a black girl with two eyes and two hands.
Just a thirteen-year-old girl with a plan.

Someday, I might want to be famous,
Become the greatest superstar known to man.
Or I might tuck away with a cat and a book,
In my own little fairy-tale land.

Why do people want to change their looks?
Life's a story, yet they rewrite their books,
Or a journey, yet they restart their cars.
Rather take a spaceship and fly it to Mars!

But this right here is me,
This right here is who I am.
May not be adorned with extravagant glam.
I'm imperfect, flaw-full, unique
And, in my opinion, there's nothing more important to seek.

Helens Kiakonda (13)
Blackfen School For Girls, Sidcup

Good Girls

Beth, Ruby and Annie, a trio so bold,
Their lives take unexpected paths, as we're told.

From Suburban moms to a life of crime,
They navigate challenges one step at a time.
With humour and heart the show will enthrall,
As they face danger, consequences and all.

Their bond grew stronger, through thick and thin,
Facing obstacles with a mischievous grin.
Each episode leaves you wanting more,
As their stories unfold right to the core.

So, grab some popcorn, settle in your seat,
'Good Girls' on Netflix is truly a treat.
You'll laugh, you'll gasp, you'll feel the thrill.
As their adventures unfold, they never stand still.

Anaum Khan (14)
Blackfen School For Girls, Sidcup

My Little Gremlin

I've got this little gremlin, her name is Lula-Rae,
she's so annoying when she doesn't get her way,
but she flashes a little smile that makes everything okay.
My little gremlin is cheeky and always wants to play,
she wrecks my room, but I let her stay.
You see, my gremlin, she's not what you think,
she's not all green and slimy, she doesn't even stink.
My little gremlin is human, she's cute and petite,
she's a small version of me, even down to her feet.
My little gremlin is perfect in every way,
she's my little sister, she really makes my day.

Lily Edwards (13)
Blackfen School For Girls, Sidcup

Bass

In the mirror's gaze, I sit and look at me.
No mask, no pretence, who is she?
With flaws and blemishes, all I see?
The beauty in my authenticity.

I am a canvas of my own stories, both old and new.
In all my lines and scars, my canvas grew.
I've weathered storms and skies bright blue.
Each page an indication, to all I've been through.

In tearshed and laughter, I find my grace.
Trying to be me, I've made my place.
With each step I take, I set my pace.
Now I'm done, let me play my bass.

Pema Sherpa (14)
Blackfen School For Girls, Sidcup

Identity Crisis

Brown hair,
Long stares,
Mum thinks I'm everywhere.
But I'm merely just a girl in her room,
Trying to figure how I am one of two.
She speaks Hungarian,
He speaks Spanish.
But, to me, it's all mumbles of gibberish.
How can I not understand what I'm supposed to?
Am I doing what I was told to do?
My brother and sister understand better than me,
He speaks fluently and she seems more Ecuadorean than I'll ever be.
Brown hair,
Long stares,
Who am I?

Sophia Montano (13)
Blackfen School For Girls, Sidcup

Let Yourself Bloom

I imagine how it would be if day feared night
I would never gaze at the moon
And if flowers were terrified of light
I could never watch them bloom

If water had a fear of heights
Gorgeous waterfalls wouldn't exist
And my favourite birds that feared taking their flights
Would have not a clue what they missed

And while I am scared of being me
I would never get to know
All of the things that were destined for me
If only I let myself grow.

Lola O'shea-Britton (12)
Blackfen School For Girls, Sidcup

This Is Me Poem

I am a museum of memories.
My brain is a wasteland of things I wish I'd said,
and my mouth is a race track of things my brain can't say.
My scars are reminders of things I've suffered and survived,
yet my cuts and bruises are things I'm trying to overcome.
No one is perfect,
but that's what makes everyone so imperfectly perfect in
their own unique way.
I am me and that is how it has to be.

Phoenix Newton-Gunstone (13)
Blackfen School For Girls, Sidcup

Anaemia's Whispers

In dawn's embrace,
The alarm clock rings,
Anaemia's fatigue,
A weight that clings,
Early mornings,
A struggle to rise,
Stressful whispers,
Beneath tired eyes,
In pale shadows,
Fatigue takes hold,
Anaemia's whispers,
A story untold,
Drained and weary,
I long for release,
Seeking strength in this battle,
Until I find peace.

Alanna Fitzpatrick (13)
Blackfen School For Girls, Sidcup

Love

I love dance
Dance makes me happy.
Dance brings peace.
Dance brings me happiness.

I love my family.
Family makes me happy.
Family makes me laugh.
Family brings happiness to me.

I love my dog.
My dog makes me happy.
My dog brings happiness to me.
My dogs make me feel safe.

Isabel Gibson (12)
Blackfen School For Girls, Sidcup

Water, Water Everywhere

Water, water, everywhere,
To wash my hands and wash my hair,
It's nice to drink anywhere,
Drink and slurp nice and good,
It comes from mountains that you don't know,
It comes from mountains, don't you know?
Falls in rain and also snow.

Zara Rahmani (12)
Blackfen School For Girls, Sidcup

What Makes Me Happy

What makes me happy,
is my money.
Oh so exciting,
with its power,
it can buy what we wish,
and desire.
It shows our happiness that
we can inspire,
but, in the end,
it's all a dream that
we wish and desire.

Karina Man (12)
Blackfen School For Girls, Sidcup

Oranges

The sweet, fluorescent smell of oranges blessed my nostrils.
A sudden wave of sweet memories washed through me.
One single bite was all it took
The old days felt like they were simply hours ago.
It was like she was still with us.

Lillie Dishart (12)
Blackfen School For Girls, Sidcup

This Is Me

My name is Daisy
I am sporty.
I play for a football team and academy
I also play cricket
I played for County U11s and I had my trials last month
I got through to the next round
I also play for Coggeshall Cricket Club
young lads are also called Coggeshall Spinners.
We are unbeaten this year
we won our league.
Now that cricket season is over
I play hockey and football.
I play hockey at school and used to play for Colchester
Hockey Club
I have been playing for around six years now
I like the sport a lot and I'm not going to give up on it.
It is also football season and I train for it
Thursday night, Friday night,
and my games are Saturday and Sunday.
I like playing sports
as they make me feel relieved and free
it is like an escape route from reality.
I love running with the breeze brushing on my feet,
I love running on Astro with a ball at my feet,

I love the phrase wicketball
at 4 or 6 o'clock
but the thing I love most is
the people who support me.

Daisy MacLaren (12)
Gosfield School, Gosfield

Young Tate

In England lived young Tate
He was loving, with his family
He speared every bit of accomplishment
When he had the ups and downs
He didn't know what to do
He woke up every day
To wonder what to do
He had a look for food
He didn't think it through
He had to go to school
But he didn't do well
He got told off four times
And wondered, *what did I do?*
He knows what he did
Now on the bus
He thought it through
He got off the bus
He was very stroppy
When he got home
He looked at his room
He had a weird idea
He immediately went to sleep
So he couldn't do his homework
So, his mum got stroppy
And started to yell

He was awoken
And was very angry
But then
Mum said
It wasn't homework
It was dinner.
"Oh, I am sorry,
I was a little tired."

Tate Buckley (11)
Gosfield School, Gosfield

Stress And Anxiety

S   tress is a cloud following me around
T   rying to crack a code into my brain
R   epeating a fast-paced sound
E   erie, creepy, knocked by a crane
S   leeping; once alive, now dead
S   weeping happiness from my head

A   nxiety is all my memory hoards
N   ever running away with my thoughts
D   riving a racecar round my mind

A   nxiety is like an everlasting build-up to a surprise
N   ever happening but so surreal
X   ylophone sounds banging on my mind like the FBI
I   magination clouded, confused, cautious
E   arly in the morning
T   ill late at night
Y   et will never end, even with all my might.

Henry Baker (13)
Gosfield School, Gosfield

I Am

I am the sound of engines roaring and planes soaring
I am the feeling of exhilaration as you fly in the air
I am the price of all of this
I am climate change
I am the melting ice caps
I am the wildfires
I am the endangered homes of species
I am all of this and so much more
I am flooding
I am the one who steals homes and lives
I am this, but you can stop this
I am climate change

I have chosen this
because I am feeling so sorry for the animals and people
who are losing their homes and lives.
We should all try to help this in any way.

George Halgh (12)
Gosfield School, Gosfield

Hero

H   is mentality will inspire generations of nervous, scared children. His heroic, fearless presence will help millions. His elegance will save many more.

E   xperienced and calm, he doesn't feel any pressure. Pure excitement, watching my role model succeed, a real-life superhero there couldn't be.

R   estricted by nothing, he is the greatest. He always had hope, and he gave it to me. Fearless and confident, he inspired me.

O   f course, he is the best there will ever be, feeling no pressure, he made me better. Ronaldo, the saviour of me. He is my hero.

Jake Barrow (13)
Gosfield School, Gosfield

This Is Me...

This is me...
Everlasting happiness with hoodies and family,
Dreams of Maverick and cricket,
Exciting science and amazing maths,

This is me...
An only childhood,
With dreams of siblings,
Joyful online friends,

This is me...
An addictive gamer with a love called 'war thunder',
Waiting for the weekend every day,
Hoping for no homework every lesson,

This is me...
Don't let mean people waste your time,
Treat people how you want to be treated,
You are you for a reason, why change yourself?

Jack Bennett (12)
Gosfield School, Gosfield

One Day In July

A day of heat,
A day of importance
One opponent to defeat
With a good performance
Starting strong,
Two quick wickets
Don't go wrong
In front of all the tickets
Resistance in the middle
Something must break
It's like a riddle
A lot at stake
All done, fifty overs gone
Now a job with bat to be done
To create the perfect swansong
Under the evening sun
Starting badly, need a partnership
Two men create one
They steady the ship
And we've won!
By the barest of margins!

Finlay Jackson (13)
Gosfield School, Gosfield

The Famous Football Fixture

F eelings of anxiety on everyone's faces, the men take to the luscious green grass.

O vercrowded with fans, the stadium alights for one of the biggest games ever.

O ceans of pressure rest on these players' shoulders.

T o win this game was like winning a ginormous trophy.

B ut if you lost, the gutting feeling would be with you for life.

A nd a tsunami of angry fans would fall on your team like a tidal wave.

L ike it or not, this game is everything.

L ife or death can depend on it.

Sonnie Thompson-Arnold (13)

Gosfield School, Gosfield

Reality Of Sports

I hate the feeling of failure,
I prefer a victory instead,
The feelings of self-doubt,
All muddle in my head,
Oh, how I just want to be the best,
The best that I can be,
I'm submerging in my thoughts,
That all just glare at me,
I'm trying my hardest,
I'm trying to think cheerful instead,
But every time I overthink,
I can't stop, feel stressed,
This commitment is too much,
All my muscles are starting to ache,
The self-doubt is growing,
Whilst I'm just trying to stay awake.

Freya MacAllan (13)
Gosfield School, Gosfield

A Day Of Racing At An Event

Rigging at my camper
gust of wind flying across my face
the sensation of how fun it is going to be today
my coach comes over to my camper and
he helps me get in the mindset for the day of racing.
My coach gets everyone in our group together and
we talk about the conditions and
how it is going to be very difficult.
Me and my friend wait in a queue
that feels like it is taking forever
but I get to the front and I am eager to go out and
I feel very confident
that I am going to do very well.

Ryan Surguy (12)
Gosfield School, Gosfield

Mountain Bike Ride

The feeling of mountain biking
flying through the air
the wind against my helmet
then, landing on the floor
hearing the suspension going *pshh*,
then, rising back up
the adrenaline rushing through my body
as I swerve through trees,
doing a wheelie down the hill
nearly losing control,
up another jump
whipping the back of my bike through the air while flying,
then, landing.
Going downhill to the next jump
feeling relaxed and enjoying the ride.
MTB is life.

Ben Bidowell (12)
Gosfield School, Gosfield

Emotions

Always feeling nervous,
with no words to speak,
anxiety getting the best of me.
On edge all the time.
With nerves running through my veins
emotions in my brain,
thinking of what's next to come,
with always wanting to call Mum,

should I go or not?
With my stomach feeling funny.
Always wanted to make money,
fearful about later life
emotions, emotions, emotions,
always messing with my head.
But, in the end, it's alright.

Mia Sewell (13)
Gosfield School, Gosfield

Never Give Up

Hi, my name is Lily,
my dream career when I'm older is to
be a professional footballer,
I also love tag rugby,
and netball,
I get bullied for loving football, but I
don't care,
I will carry on with my dream.
To all the football lovers who are
being pressured to stop following your
dream, don't listen, carry on, no one
will care,
never give up your dream,
this is me,
this is you.

Lily Ripper
Gosfield School, Gosfield

A Whole New World

My VR headset. A whole new world.
When I put on those goggles, I never hurl
when you want to escape, the headset always awaits
like an Aladdin's cave, there are so many games
but the only issue is that you have to have paid
oh, beat sabre with those swords of light
I'll be playing that game into the night
the headset calls me like a moth to a light
but those headset marks give me an awful fright.

Poppy Brooks (13)
Gosfield School, Gosfield

Rugby

When you step on that field with your friends
who are willing to protect you
the feeling is unmatched.
Rugby is my passion that comes with challenges,
injuries and hard work.
That is put into it
running around for eighty minutes isn't easy
plus, sometimes, the pitch is as muddy as a pigsty
which gives you burns and grassy, muddy legs.
Lastly, I hope to be a pro rugby player when I'm older.

William Foxton (12)
Gosfield School, Gosfield

Oh, Badminton

Oh! Badminton,
Oh! Badminton
what a wonderful game
from the highs
to the lows

but when I lose, I just keep trying
when I lose
I grow
to be better and better.

Oh! Badminton,
Oh! Badminton,
the shuttle flies towards me,
like a plane in the sky,
strike!
It flies the other way,
boom!
What a wonderful game!
Oh! Badminton.

Thomas Loring (13)
Gosfield School, Gosfield

This Is Me!

Karen O, like a role model to me
I hold my snake Hatshepsut like I'm the calmest person in the world.
I chase my dog round the garden like a demented horse.
I speak Spanish like I can tackle anything.
I draw and write about Egyptians all day long like I'm a historian.
I'm brave like a lion and loyal like a dog
I'm proud and merry like a lynx and as enthusiastic as a butterfly.

Bella Bown (10)
Gosfield School, Gosfield

Keep Calm And Carry On

With a deep breath in and a deep breath out,
hiding your emotions is not the way out,
tell an adult, your teacher too,
because the long, windy path has no clue.
With ups, having a wonderful day
and downs maybe leading you astray.
As my poem comes to an end,
you will know there will always be a friend,
use this poem to calm you down,
and smile instead of having a frown.

Freddie Paul (12)
Gosfield School, Gosfield

This Is Me

Nobody can judge *me*,
My appearance is *me*,
Nobody can judge my beliefs, it's *me*,
My emotions are different, it's *me*,
I don't care if anyone likes me, that's fine, but this is *me*,
My goals are different to others than *me*,
I want to be the better version of *me*,

This is *me*.

Austin Thompson-Arnold (11)
Gosfield School, Gosfield

This Is Me

This is me,
Not ordinary
My fingers of six
My hair blacker than a void
Unique for sure
Different, no doubt

I'm tired of the ways that things have been,
I hide from
The ugly truth,
That poisons me like a spider.

I put on a fake smile every day,
To hide my emotions
But that's just who I am
This is me.

Aryan Popat (11)
Gosfield School, Gosfield

My Opinion

This is just my opinion,
but,
I should speak up,
I would never say,
keep my feelings to myself
I should always
try my best in everything I do
it's so silly to say,
"I'm not important,"
so, I should remember that
I am enough
I would never think
I can't do it
but
this is just my opinion.

Tallulah Holder (11)
Gosfield School, Gosfield

Me

A game of chess, so hard.
A video game, so quick.
A bed, no time to use.

A world so mean and dark
A light so bright and nice
A song so loud and long

A world in a computer
A cube in the world
A square in the cube

Break the loop of society
But you can't break the loop of life
A toy made by light.

Jack Fower (14)
Gosfield School, Gosfield

This Is Me

I find it hard to read,
I find it hard to write,
I find it hard to spell,
sometimes, it keeps me up at night,
English is not my best
but I always give it a try,
but when it comes to sports
I feel like I'm alive.
I love my buggy racing
especially when I come first,
I am so proud of myself
I feel like I could burst.

Ralph Payne (11)
Gosfield School, Gosfield

This Is Me

This is me,
I love football and was playing for Ipswich at the age of nine,
I do go-karting and am the number one,
I love rugby and I am the sponsor of Harvey Hill,
I have my own fingerprint that no one else can copy,
I am different because wouldn't it be boring if we were all the same?
This is me.

Tyler Dyer (12)
Gosfield School, Gosfield

This Is Me

I am me
But that's not all.
I am scared
Trying to hide my fears
Trying to hide me.
I can stop
Believing
I am
A failure
Never
Pushing back.
But
A nervous wreck
A slave to my fears
I am not
Able to be me
I must live my life.
This is me.

Ava Coldwell (11)
Gosfield School, Gosfield

The Thing I Like Most

The thing I like most is that bikes have been there for me
every day
after a long day
of school and I
believe that everyone should know how to ride a bike
and it doesn't matter where you
are from, you
should be able to experience that happy feeling like
when I am playing on my bike.

Tia Hance (12)
Gosfield School, Gosfield

Dancing Is My Passion

D ancing is my favourite thing to do
A lways thinking of routines to do
N ever giving up on my passion
C os I am gonna make it happen
I nspiring people every day
N ever giving up, even though I am far
G oing to become an absolute star.

Betsy Mead (13)
Gosfield School, Gosfield

This Is Me

I am Neil, I read books.
I don't know my favourite book.
But my favourite electronic is my phone.
Crisps, a snack so crispy, salty and grand.
I like to play the piano
like reading.
I am not sporty at all.
I love my bed and cannot get up in the morning.

Neil Taylor (11)
Gosfield School, Gosfield

Netball

I love netball,
nothing will stop me playing it,
it lights up my mood whenever I'm down and
it makes me happy and my family too!
But my fears sometimes take over and
my nerves kick in,
but nothing will stop me from trying to win!

Ava Johnson (12)
Gosfield School, Gosfield

Cow Man

He is strong, I am not,
She does good, I try to,
He has a dog, I have a cow
His dog is trained, my cow in training,
He has money but I don't,
They are them,
I am me,
I like cows, he likes dogs,
Cows make me happy.

Thomas Howie (12)
Gosfield School, Gosfield

Friends In Arms

Like stars in the sky,
that's how many friends you have nearby,
like how tall Mount Everest is,
that's how long your friendship will last,
like how every word you said,
is the amount of memories you will have extended.

Rowan Stevens (14)
Gosfield School, Gosfield

Katie's Poem

K indhearted, that is me.
A m always found playing a sport.
T he weather won't stop my play.
I will play to the end of the day.
E ven if the sun goes away.

Katie Logan (11)

Gosfield School, Gosfield

Sebby

S tringy spaghetti, mouthwatering meatballs jiggling in my mouth

E xtraordinary, enchanting, engaging, enlightening

B raveheart

B rilliant brain

Y oung lad.

Sebby Smith (11)
Gosfield School, Gosfield

This Is Me

Staring down the bowler in fear
the only feeling you can feel
when the ball is near
the tremendous flourish of the bat.

Alfie Youngs (13)
Gosfield School, Gosfield

Acrostic Swifty Poem

Dedicated to Taylor Swift songs

C all it what you want

H alf of my heart

L avender haze

O ur song

E nchanted.

Chloe Golebiowski (11)

Gosfield School, Gosfield

The History Of Cooking

A haiku

Knife, weapon of God,
Brings life to textures unknown,
In the dish of time.

Ewan Harmer (13)

Gosfield School, Gosfield

Growing Up Is A Mess

You know when people tell you you're
meant to know who you are,
but when you think about it all day, all month,
and all year,
it all starts to seem bizarre,
because you never come to an end; your thoughts,
your nightmares, your lies,
you sit and make up your myths about who you want to be,
but you know when it doesn't happen, it
won't be a surprise,
so, when people ask who you are, it just gets
so annoying,
at this point, that's all that's in your mind
the idea that the future doesn't exist,
well, maybe you don't have to think this way
well, maybe it's too early,
and while I don't know who I am or who I want to
be, I still have interests,
like art, writing, reading poetry and more, like having
a walk outside, shivering in the cold,
you too have your interests that most likely won't
be the same,
but let those interests express you, not the stress
to impress,

not the thought that when you grow up, it will all
be a mess,
I might not know about my future, or the 'real'
me,
but, so far, all of these interests will get to
express me,
so, the next time you ask someone who they
want to be,
don't put them under that pressure, for they
possibly could not know,
instead, ask them for their hobbies
things they may or may not like,
or figure it out together and stay by their side,
understand them, communicate, get what I
mean?
You may act and say no, but wouldn't you
want the same?

Kira Kazemyr (13)
Hazelwick School, Three Bridges

The Melody Of Words

Should I describe it as a summer's breeze,
gracefully crafted,
elegantly poised?
Its sharp edges crisp and neat,
the smell of enchantment between its pages,
the rocky road it sails throughout the day,
the peaceful end throughout the night.
Its wonders that never cease,
holding more knowledge,
more power,
more than any man could hold.

The newly printed pages,
the crinkle of a new story,
through every turn,
it speaks to me,
the pain that was untold.

I've travelled throughout the depths of Taurus,
seen the abyss of Hell itself,
the thorns of the fires,
the ruthlessness of shadow hunters,
all that and more,
all that's hidden in its song.

Devouring the pages,
devouring the vocabulary,
devouring the emotions and feelings,
that gleam inside.

To create a world,
a world so perfect,
it cannot be true,
but, beneath it all,
is concealed the pain and longing,
of all lost souls.

The words that show me the meaning of life,
the words that tell of the wisdom,
the great wisdom itself.
All word,
shaped into a beautiful melody,
that brings tears to my eyes.

My comfort, my joy, my happiness,
all wrapped up,
concealing the song,
the rings through my heart.

The world could end,
life destroyed,
but I will always be curled up,
on my sofa,

clutching my books,
that are, to me,
more valuable than the stars and moon themselves.

Jeevika Senthil (12)
Hazelwick School, Three Bridges

Exams: Triumphs And Trials

In the realm of examinations, where trials abound,
Triumphs and tribulations, intricately wound.
With literature as our armour and erudition as our guide.

Through sleepless vigils and ceaseless toil,
We pursue success, nurturing the soil,
Each injury a skirmish, each assessment a conflict's core,
Yet we preserve, for aspirations stand before.

The struggle is formidable, but so too is the gain,
As we surround the odds, shattering each chain.
For every ordeal that confronts our path,
Enhances our fortitude, paving the way for aftermath.

Let us not be daunted by the trials we confront,
In exams and assessments, this voyage we confront,
For when the victory is finally seized,
We shall treasure the expedition, as it has been decreed.

In accomplishments and hardships, we find our finesse,
In the quest for erudition, we locate our address,
With unwavering resolve and unwavering endeavour,
In the chronicle of examinations, we script our narrative
endeavour.

Joel Hampstead (14)
Hazelwick School, Three Bridges

Indian And Proud

I may have been British by birth but I am Indian by heart,
I feel proud to be from the nation of spices,
The country that roars with noise,
The country of vibrant colours and Rangolis,
I am proud to be an Indian.

I may have been British by birth but I am Indian by heart,
I feel proud to be from the nation with one of the best
cricket teams,
The country that makes Bollywood films,
The country that produces such phenomenal food,
I am proud to be an Indian.

I may have been British by birth but I am Indian by heart,
I feel proud to be from the nation of sarees and sherwanis,
The country of masala chai and tea,
The country that's the home of the Taj Mahal, one of the
seven beauties,
I am proud to be an Indian.

I may have been British by birth but I am Indian by heart,
I feel proud to be from the nation of such interesting history,
The country that celebrates Eid, Diwali and Holi,
The country that is home to the Ganga River,

I am proud to be an Indian.

I am proud to be from India.

Aditya Vaidya (14)
Hazelwick School, Three Bridges

Preference

I see you,
You don't see me,
I use my words,
You don't listen,
"I need your help,"
"I don't care,"
"I have mental issues,"
"Not as bad as mine,"
"I need your help!"
"Shut up!"

I don't use my words,
You say, "Speak more!"
But that's what I did before!
You tell me to shut up,
But then you want me to talk,
I cut my hair,
"I liked it longer,"
I have brown hair,
"I like blondes,"
"I like reading and football,"
"I like girly girls,"
I don't vape,
"You're no fun,"
"I like my skin the way it is,"
"Use make-up!"

"I have blue eyes like the ocean,"
"Green are better!"
"I'm tall,"
"I prefer short,"
"I like myself the way I am,"
"Change!"
As long as I'm happy, "No."

Francesca Markwick (12)
Hazelwick School, Three Bridges

This Is Me

Hi, my name is Jack
And this poem is all about me.
The base of me is my family.
My mum, dad, pets and my brother.
My cousins, auntie, uncle and grandad are also very important.
I love playing football, biking or skate park.
I also go on my Xbox a lot to play with my friends.
I am very friendly and kind towards others.
I may not be the largest of people
But that's what makes me different.
I play golf and cricket in my spare time with my dad.
I am very fun, nice and supportive.
I am always willing to go out
Even if it's just out on my street.
My football team is Devils FC
And we always try and never give up.
I like going fishing with my dad
And I love to go to the airport to watch the planes take off and land.
I also like trains.
I love going on holiday as it is very warm.
This is all about me
And I am out!

Jack Lonsdale (12)
Hazelwick School, Three Bridges

This Is Me

School is rewarding and impressive
And allows for me to be expressive,
Around me I see familiar faces
And loads of well-known places.

I express my emotions using separation,
By removing myself from the situation,
So why does it still get to me excessively?
On the inside, I'm ready to accept defeat.

However, I've got my girls around me,
And they will not allow me to slip and fall,
Into a place that does not even let you crawl.

Basically what I'm saying is
Keep your friends close,
'Cause they will not let the door close,
They will always have my back,
Stopping the pitch black.

The sunlight will always shine through the blinds,
The birds will always sing their shine,
Giving me peace of mind,
Stopping these bad thoughts hanging around for too long.

Olivia Randolph (14)
Hazelwick School, Three Bridges

I Am Me

I have a base of my family,
The people who make me, me.
They help me overcome my fears,
They help me face my problems,
They are my family.
They make me laugh,
They make me smile,
My friends are here with me to run a mile.

I am made of gymnastics,
My coaches are part of my family,
They help me see what I can't see
And help me with different moves,
They are my coaches.

My walls are made of sports,
I love to learn different things.
Reading is one of my things,
Taking me to a different world, exploring.

At my core, you will find my heart filled with kindness.
I am full of happiness,
I worry for my friends
If I don't think they're okay.

I am reliable,
You can trust me with anything.

This is me.

Vongai Musanhi (12)
Hazelwick School, Three Bridges

This Is Me

I am made of...
Kindness, care and generosity
I am strong and I am brave,
I always keep going and I do not give up.

Sometimes I am anxious,
Other times I am happy
At times I am hyper or the complete opposite... Sad.

My friends are my true heroes,
Pulling me out of dark places
When I fall down, looking after me
When I'm vulnerable.

Family is my happiness,
The light in a dark tunnel.

I am a people pleaser,
I want what's best for others,
I don't like seeing my friends unhappy.

Football is my life, where I'm my most happy,
Where my mind is at ease,
I feel nothing but pure safety.

Animals make me happy,
They are amazing creatures.

This is me, this is what I'm made of.

Mia Evans (12)
Hazelwick School, Three Bridges

Look

Why won't you look our way,
Look at our pleas, look at our tears and look at our lives
Look at us, the humans behind the stats and behind the
headlines
But you won't look our way,
You look away, you look at the money in your pockets and
the people singing your praise,
You look away from everything, selectively blind to the
privilege that lifted you in the first place,
So, go on,
Look away.
Look away from the people in pain, the people who are
overflowing from the graveyards.
'Cause if you keep looking away, eventually there won't be
anyone left to look at.
Right?
So, go on,
Look away.
Look away from the people in the streets, the people on
your doorstep.
'Cause if you don't look away, eventually you won't see it
coming your way.

Nox Collins (14)
Hazelwick School, Three Bridges

This Is Me

I am made of skin
Some people don't care and put me in the bin
At my core you will find a heart
Inside it is lovely, things like my dad playing darts.

I have a best friend
He is always there for me when I need him
That's what's so great about him
He supports me when things look grim.

Another thing that makes my heart so pure
Is some special people called my family
I love them oh so very much
And I love a subject called geography.

I can be dumb
I can be smart
I also can be quite funny
And oh, don't forget I'm Pakistani.

I love my family
I love my friends
I love everything that makes me pure
And they are the wondrous cure.

Sami Amin (12)
Hazelwick School, Three Bridges

Harmony Of My Life

In the mirror's gaze, I see my face,
A fifteen-year-old, running life's race,
Confident mind, humble at heart,
In the journey of life, I'm ready to start.

Ambitions and hopes twinkle distantly like stars,
Guiding us beyond Earthly bars,
I yearn for a future, both bright and grand,
Where my dreams and destiny stand.

My guitar is more than just an instrument,
A friend, a companion, a sentiment,
A medium of self-expression,
A way to escape from the mundane and the tension.

The thrill of a tackle, the joy of a goal,
In this world of football, we find our soul,
In this beautiful game, we're forever entwined,
With the spirit of unity, our hearts are aligned.

Shrey Mathur (15)
Hazelwick School, Three Bridges

The Bricks That Made Me

These were the bricks that made me...
When I was young I was the tallest, most magnificent
building in the city,
but I would still look up to people.
As I got older this once beautiful building that had so much
future started to rot and decay as everyone else grew
stronger and taller.
When everyone had dreams on their mind I was there,
Sat thinking about what brick would crumble next,
But my loved one kept on encouraging me to stay
and then the bricks I lost started to appear again
and I was the tallest building again.
This town will always be my city
and my house will always be my home
so just don't worry if you're alone.

Yan Olsen (12)
Hazelwick School, Three Bridges

I'm Freya A In The Place To Be

I'm Freya A in the place to be
I'm the oldest swimmer in my class
Yet I always get there last.
I'm Freya A in the place to be
And thanks to rainbow magic I can play flute in Grade 3.
I'm Freya A in the place to be
I watch my cartoons and I read my books just to escape
reality.
I'm Freya A in the place to be
My middle name is Greatl and I'm proud of it too
It's after my grandma who survived World War Two.
She died a few months ago
Chloe helped me get through the tears
All my other friends disappeared.
I'm Freya A in the place to be
I'm not much but I'm me.

Freya A (12)
Hazelwick School, Three Bridges

All In The Name Of God

Do gods look at their sinners
in the way mothers look at their children?
Why does she look at my sister
like she's born to be a serial killer?

Why is it that she views my sister's love
as something that must be gone for good?
What hurts is my mother kills with so much love
she's willing to clean up my sister's pool of blood

my sister did nothing wrong, that was true
yet so many bodies, like her, turned blue
none of it was paint, all only the works of their skins
the skin that the parents didn't let them breathe in.

Onyx Burden (14)
Hazelwick School, Three Bridges

Who Are You?

Are you the experiences throughout your life,
A combination of happy lives, sadness and strife
Or are you the way you were born?
Destiny written at the start,
Fated to live your simple life until the day you part
Or perhaps you are a mixture of both?
Writing destiny yourself with years of growth
And instilled with morals on your day of birth
That never break throughout your time on Earth.
You can choose whatever you believe,
It doesn't matter what others perceive.
If we let people believe what they want
Everyone will be happy for once.

Michael Hill (14)
Hazelwick School, Three Bridges

I Am...

Identity is a beautiful thing,
A unique blend of heart and mind,
A symphony of passions, dreams and fears,
Shaping who I am.

I am not my age or the colour of my hair,
I am all the books I read,
I am my thoughts and all the words I speak,
I am my laughter and every tear I cry.

I am not a height or weight,
I am the places I've been and the one I call home,
I am the things I believe in
And the people I love.

Identity is who we are, deep down inside.
A journey of discovery and a tapestry of stories and beauty.

Abigail Flynn (14)
Hazelwick School, Three Bridges

Pressure

Pressure.
I'm crumbling under the idea of perfection.
Mistakes are a part of life
But I always want to get it right.
Why is 99% not good enough?
Why do I always have to strive for 100%?

Pressure.
I'm putting all this weight on my shoulders
Expecting myself to always get it right.
But that is impossible.
I'm learning it's okay to make mistakes.
Not everything has to be perfect.
I don't need to be disappointed when I get it wrong.
Mistakes are not my enemy.
They will only help me get better.

Kayley White (15)
Hazelwick School, Three Bridges

Who Am I?

I am someone who is anxious about my childhood ending and adulthood beginning.
I am someone who puts others before myself and has too much empathy.
I come from a Pakistani family, one that never forgets its traditions.
I come from a British community, one that is kind, compassionate and accepting.
I wish to pursue art and study a profession with it.
I wish to learn how to cook and nostalgia will be my key ingredient.
I am... I am thankful for the people who surround me and for those who have helped build me.
I couldn't be any more grateful.

Faizaan Khan (12)
Hazelwick School, Three Bridges

I Am... Me

A puzzle solver - I solve the hardest puzzles,
Connecting the pieces that don't fit.

Hardworking - I work all day,
Making sure it is perfect in a way.

Religious - I am. My belief taped to my heart,
It stays with me, never apart.

An Asian I am. I'm proud to be one,
A Sri Lankan to be exact, a country in the sun.

Independent - I am, but not always.
I can find my way but sometimes I am a bit dependent.

Unique - I am. I guess everyone is,
Yes, you heard it... Me and you.

Zaid Mohamed (12)
Hazelwick School, Three Bridges

Identity

I may be young but I know my identity.
I am loud and extroverted
But sometimes I feel the opposite
I am grateful and forgiving
And I am a seeker of knowledge, forever curious
But surely 'identity' means more than that.

To me, it is about my achievements, hopes and dreams
The way my creative mind thinks,
My passions, and my hates.

My identity is carefully written day by day
Like an unfinished book
But it is a unique story
And I am proud to be the author.

Jasmin Byrne (14)
Hazelwick School, Three Bridges

Time

Hello,
I am time.
You've probably never seen me before.
That's fine,
I walk alone,
sometimes quickly
so fast that people don't see me.
Sometimes very slow,
people want me to fly by
anyway,
I am a shape-shifter,
a shadow,
a dream or a nightmare,
nevertheless,
once I'm gone, I'm gone.
Time never turns back,
so, keep happy moments in your heart
the bad ones taken out
time never comes back.
So, enjoy me while you can.

Khanak Tiwari (12)
Hazelwick School, Three Bridges

I'm Not Her

I'm not that little girl,
The little girl who would jump at your arrival,
The little girl who was so eager to go to school.

She was fighting a losing battle,
She gave everything her all.

I'm not that little girl,
Who wasn't afraid,
The little girl
Who wasn't alone.

She was blinded by lies of the real world
And constantly walked on eggshells.

I wish I could tell her one thing,
I'm proud of you.

Ellie Thompson (15)
Hazelwick School, Three Bridges

This Is Me

This is me,
I am proud to be me,
I love rugby and dance,
That's what makes me who I am.

I love my family,
They've helped me at my lowest,
I love my dog,
I miss my cat,
I'll love them forever more.

My friends are my life,
I couldn't do it without them,
They are my ride-or-die
And I'll always love them.

I am caring,
I am kind,
I always try my best
And I'll never give up.

Olivia-Grace Weaver (12)
Hazelwick School, Three Bridges

Shine Bright

Dancing is a passion,
A passion which is mine.
And when you walk on that stage,
Happiness grows inside you.
Nothing can stop you
From doing what you love.
Confidence embraces you,
Like a soft gentle hug.
In the spotlight,
You shine bright.
Never give up,
As dreams come true.
Great achievements happen under the spotlight
So shine bright, keep believing
And show the world what you are capable of.

Abi Dodd (14)
Hazelwick School, Three Bridges

This Is Me

I am happy and excited for everything,
My family, they are supportive,
They care for me,
They are what made me, me.
I can be shy,
I can be loud,
I can be funny,
I can be annoying,
I am kind,
I am thoughtful,
I am positive,
I am curious.
I dream to explore,
See beautiful landscapes
And the most vivid animals
And the most spectacular landmarks.
This is me!

Daniel Bowen (12)
Hazelwick School, Three Bridges

About Me

Who am I?
Who are you?
Everything I say is true.
I'm a dancer,
Are you?
My favourite colour is blue,
How about you?
My biggest fear is spiders,
I've only touched a few,
Also, there are heights,
Whatever should I do?
How about you?
My dream is to become an actress,
How about you?
Do you wanna be one too?
Everyone is so rude,
Whatever will I do?

Eleanor Shaw (12)
Hazelwick School, Three Bridges

This Is Me, Who Am I?

What makes me, me?
View me as you like.
In this world, you see
Lots of me look alike.

Bitter words that cause arguments
To stand out in the crowd.
Standing in Parliament,
What is this about?

Music that gets me moving
Like fireworks that spark,
As I start grooving,
The journey, on I embark.

Let it be!
No one else is like me!

Alice Fu (14)
Hazelwick School, Three Bridges

This Is Me

I'm thankful for my family
Even though sometimes it can end in tragedy
I'm thankful for my friends
Because my smiling never seems to end.

Religion is important to me
It's like a daily cup of tea
I have extraordinary skills
That could even pay the bills.

My house is where I live
It has my old sieve
I am free
This is me.

Aila Jaufferdeen (12)
Hazelwick School, Three Bridges

Religion

Some call it religion, for others, it's a way of life,
Those without knowledge may find it a restricting boundary
between life and freedom.
Those with knowledge perceive it as divine enlightenment.
John 3:16, the word of honour,
Those lost come from wonder,
Scriptures and testaments,
Prayers and worship,
Allow you to know Jehovah God.

Violet Mazanzi (14)
Hazelwick School, Three Bridges

How About...?

How about mixed race? Is that the phrase?
How about dual heritage? Is that a phrase?
How about stop looking at people in interracial relationships and judging them?
How about stop being homophobic?
How about stop being racist?
How about stop being Islamophobic?
How about just stop being offensive?
How about that?

Theo Ranganathan (14)
Hazelwick School, Three Bridges

What I Like To Do

M y favourite things to do are play football and many other sports.

A mbitions are to become an engineer and to do all sorts.

Q ueues take forever but it's worth the roller coaster to fly like a bird.

I 'm a student and love to learn.

L et me be who I am and I'll let you be you!

Maqil Zawahir (12)
Hazelwick School, Three Bridges

This Is Me

T rust in family
H elpfulness towards everyone
I slam is my religion
S uccesses and achievements.

I dentity and appearance
S kills I've learnt.

M orals I go by
E thnicity and race.

Ayaan Goraya (12)

Hazelwick School, Three Bridges

Identity

I think to myself,
Who am I?

Am I an individual
Or am I my job?
Do I have ambitions
Or am I ambitionless?
Am I alone
Or do I have friends?
Who am I?

Does anyone really know?
I think to myself.

Julian Szmulka
Hazelwick School, Three Bridges

This Is Me

I am Grace
Sometimes people can misunderstand me
But I am the nicest person you can find
We have the most fun times together

I am a horse rider and with this job you have to stay strong
If they kick you off
Stand proud
Stay loyal, don't try to run away
Get back on
Saddle up
And gallop away

In school I have to stay organised otherwise you will be
there for more than six hours
I work hard, that's why I'm smart
I'm confident in school but my spelling can take me back
I'm creative and kind so don't mind
I've been through such difficult times
You're not the only one

At home I'm in a new world
Most of the time I'm lazy but
I do what I'm told
At home I have a dog called Poppy
And a hamster called Snowdrop
They're the best you can buy

They're loving
Caring
Crazy, so don't mind
They're also loving pets
We are very adventurous in a way
We spend summer days riding bikes, flying kites and no one gets into fights
Sandy beaches, hot or cold
We are never getting old
We never give up
We push ourselves to the limit
That's the Kingstons

So back to me
Let's get this straight
I'm fearless
I'm passionate
I'm proud of what I do
So if you're reading this that means I have made it into a book
So I will leave the rest to you
Finish your story
And write your ending
Also, before I go I just wanted to say...
Be yourself!

Grace Kingston (11)
Hornchurch High School, Hornchurch

What's Important To Me

T his is a poem about what I really love and appreciate
H ere is the first thing I love, axolotls because they are cute
E very Friday I look forward to seeing my dad

G ames are how I spend my afternoons
A fter all I find games entertaining
L ater in the day I listen to some music and then I go to sleep
A fter I wake up I have a cup of coffee
R ight after I arrive at school and I look for my friends
I look forward to drama because I find it fun
A long with hunting the Galarian Birds on Pokémon Go
N othing means more to me than my mum and dad

B eginning of the afternoon I have painted some Warhammer
I t would mean a lot to me if I found Galarian Birds
R egarding the weekend, I stay in and watch movies
D efinitely enjoy helping my friends
S o here is my poem, thanks for reading!

Danny-Junior Kelly (13)
Hornchurch High School, Hornchurch

The Outsider

To you in the mirror at dusk,
Is it the real me, who is the simple wallflower?
One who recites conversational lines in their own brain,
A creature that stands staring from the outside looking in.

Eyes adjusting to the light and common sights from the
cruel darkness,
Things are not quite what they seem.
A chronically exhausted observer chronicles its negative
experiences,
Puts it in a little pile to catalogue its battles and poisons.

A silhouette of the unsightly gains sentience from flesh and
bones,
And remains shut outside the door.
Eternally trapped inside the confines of its own unorthodox
universe.
Such a morbid thing such as that should never be
unwelcomed inside,
It should be left outside in the thunder and rain, a tribute to
old times.

For that is who I think I am.

Eta Joshi (14)
Hornchurch High School, Hornchurch

Me

This is me
I am sometimes quite lonely
But not to worry
I always put family and friends in front of me.

I will keep on blowing bubbles until I can't any more
My dreams I hope will not fade and die
My fortunes are always hiding
I look everywhere
I'll guess I'll keep on blowing bubbles, pretty bubbles in the air.

My grandad and me are for life besties
Sometimes I see him in my dreams
The best grandad a boy could want
He supports me no matter what
The main thing we have in common is our love for the claret and blue army.

I love to collect things so here is a list:
Number one is Lego and bricks
Number two is footie kits
Number three is a lot of West Ham bits!

Back to this is me
I'm as funny as Mr Smee

And of course, as friendly as can be
This is me!

Jack Bailey
Hornchurch High School, Hornchurch

Who I Am

B ritish and loud and proud, give me all your fish and chips

L ove my mum Rosie too, she is my best friend and she makes me smile and I also love my family

A cting is my dream, one day standing in front of a big crowd and winning awards

C ancer is my zodiac sign, I'm a stereotypical Cancer it's true, July the 14th is the day I celebrate

K ind, outgoing, clever, funny, calm and very shy - that's me and it's what I am proud to be

P urple is my favourite colour but I also like teal and mint green

I get annoyed quickly but forgive even quicker, I also get mad very quickly but also forgive

N o day at school is a good day for me, I wish school was more fun

K -Pop is my life, I love to listen to it all day and night. Blackpink is the best.

Courtney Cross (12)

Hornchurch High School, Hornchurch

This Is Me

This is me, I am Joan
I am quiet and I am tall
I like music, I like my friends
The music is most of the noise in my head
I think a lot
I think though too much noise just makes me mute
I like to narrate my life like I'm in a big, fat book
I like movies, I don't read
People say I'm pretty but that's what they see
I'm insecure and a bit more tall
But that is okay

The music calms me down even if it's loud
I'm always confused but that's who I am
I use my phone a bit too much but that's okay, I'm not isolated
I'm not isolated from my friends, I study and I'm human
I am quiet but I am loud
There are so many reasons why but I still do not know why
I am Joan and I am twelve
And this is me closing this poem.

Joan Ukpokolo (12)
Hornchurch High School, Hornchurch

How Do I Feel?

Every day people make new comments about me.
"You're too kind."
"People are gonna take advantage of you."
Maybe I am kind
I can't help it
The guilt inside me kills me every time
Can I be better?
Is there something wrong with me?
I have always wanted to become a lawyer
I'm stubborn
I love history and I'm good at decorating
My passion is Bhangra, on top of that Karan Aujla
Music calms me down when I'm angry or when my OCD
kicks in
My zodiac sign is Taurus
I love going to weddings and meeting extended family
But sometimes my cousins frustrate me
Constantly telling me I'm wrong
Even as a joke it hurts
They say I can't take a joke
Well, maybe it wouldn't hurt if they learned how to make
one!

Ashmeet Kaur (12)
Hornchurch High School, Hornchurch

A Poem All About Me

God can help me when I'm feeling blue
but on the bright side, He made a peaceful world
including cows that go moo
football to make me feel good
but imagine if the ball was made out of wood
my family has a really high-quality chair
and my little sister has an intimidating stare
with a family that's all about me
and I am happy with my friendly tree
me as a grateful boy
I'm joyful for the things my parents do
my way of saying great means a lot

G   enerous
R   esilient
E   nthusiastic
A   spirational
T   houghtful

I can aspire, believe and achieve in all my classes and clubs
if I work to the best of my ability
you will see me on the pitch
alongside Tom, Hunt and Mitch.

Teddy Thompson (11)
Hornchurch High School, Hornchurch

This Is Me

This is me
A peaceful, steady stream that's aglow
Soft, soothing, comforting
A joy to see.

As hard as a rock
As light as a feather
My heart is compassionate for those who seek luck
I try my best for those who are stuck.

Intriguing, happy, energetic
These words flow through my body
Showing to the crowd
Never letting down.

Jaeleen, a beacon of strength and grace
In a world that tries to put her in place
Her resilience shines like a guiding light
Defying expectations with every step she takes.

This is me
A peaceful, steady stream
With a compassionate heart
Showing the the crowd and never letting down
This is me
A happy girl with big dreams.

Jaeleen Ofosu (11)
Hornchurch High School, Hornchurch

Who Am I?

I'm a girl who loves
Rainbows, unicorns and sparkles.
But do I really? No. So let's get to the real
Thing. My name's Joyce and I love a lot of things
Actually starting with my family. Because without my family,
Especially my parents, I wouldn't be here right now. Like
literally... I love
God more than I love cod. You know, like fish and chips and
I really like fish and chips.
I want to be nice and rich when I'm older, carrying a lot of
cars on my shoulder
I love my Nigerian culture and their food too.
Don't forget I love watermelon
I love watching Netflix in my warm, comfy bed.
But I guess I'm going to have to end
It here because it's getting kind
Of dead.

Joyce Amusan (12)
Hornchurch High School, Hornchurch

Believe In Yourself

For me this is what I want to be
Opening my eyes, I felt like I wanted to cry
Running my fingers through my hair,
Even I wanted to disappear.
Nothing would change until I started to take action,
Science called to me, you should have seen my reaction!
I watch CSI and all those kinds of shows
Crying, I said, "I want to do this the most!"
Singing and dancing with a kick in my step
Cheering and laughing I found my safe space
I wanted to stay, I wanted people to see my face
Eventually, I made this for life
No one could help me more
Creating my own path finally really helped my case
Everyone can find their purpose if they look hard enough
Look at me, even I have had luck!

Zipporah Gokhul (12)
Hornchurch High School, Hornchurch

Life's Sonnet

At my core you shall find a soul burning with passion
A collector of skills: confident in his ability
Cripples around others, suffers social anxiety
Stands up for himself, doesn't take gossip politely

Has no favourite gender or flavour, enjoys all equality
Hates idolising people: not into celebrities
Behaves towards others kindly, with empathy
Always anxious and worries about the future shoddily

Yet his walls once high and mighty have begun to wither
Fissures formed and emotions leaked
Heals self through seeing the world with a pencil
Ambitions burn like eternal flames powering him

In this story, I'm the author
For this is my life after all.

Syed Shah (13)
Hornchurch High School, Hornchurch

What Makes Me Me?

Here's a poem about the bricks that built my walls
They may be thin but they will never fall
Family is my base
A very strong one too
They are the people I never want to lose
Some things I like to watch are the Beta Squad, Side Men,
Marvel, The Hunger Games and Netflix
These things may not be your cup of tea but they are mine
If you don't like it, keep it to yourself, please
I love games, trampolining and cooking
I'm very passionate about these things
What about you?
What do you like to do?
My favourite time of year is Christmas
I love the feel, weather, cosiness, music and food
What about you?
When's your favourite time of year, dude?

Harvey Irish-Jones (12)
Hornchurch High School, Hornchurch

Family For Life

F ishing with my dad wasn't that bad
A nimals are cute so I own a few
M y mum is the best, I'll provide for her next
I care for my friends even though they are a mess
L ove I receive,
Y es, love I'll give

F amily is strong together and hopefully forever
O bsession with art but it is so hard
R eplacing stuff I didn't know would be tough

L iving off my parents after all they are my carers
I nfluence I was supposed to be not like I wanted to be
F ighting with my brother and arguing even further
E xcitement and joy ever since I was a little boy.

Alexander Kraster (13)

Hornchurch High School, Hornchurch

This Is Me

I   nterested in fashion, cooking and music
S   adness overtakes me whenever I don't have time to finish something
A   bility to adjust to any situation
B   eneficial things help me thrive in life
E   xtroverted when around new people
L   oves spending time with family
L   ikes to annoy my little brother
E   ager to learn new things and to help anyone I can

At my core you will find a love for music and cooking
You will also find a desire to become an architect and interior designer
My family means everything to me
Without them I wouldn't be the independent girl I am today.

Isabelle Gjoni-Rakipaj (12)
Hornchurch High School, Hornchurch

Me And My Family And School

Hello, I'm Tomilola
I'm eleven years old
I'm the third oldest in my family
I have two siblings
I have a mum and a dad
My date of birth is January 30th
My favourite seasons are summer and winter
I like Christmas because you get presents and good food
The reason I like school is so you can study and pass your GCSEs
School is very important because you learn well
You can then have a very nice life by getting a job and paying your bills
Even though you don't like school
It doesn't mean that you shouldn't go to school
It will help you get a good life
So just enjoy yourself.

Tomilola Hassan (11)
Hornchurch High School, Hornchurch

This Is Me

D aring, I will take on any challenge, even a risky one and overcome it

E very day I will work hard and become the best

S mart, I know what to do and how to do it

I n the future I want to be very successful

G ame designer is what I'll be and if you challenge me I will win

N ever give up is what I'll do, I can't be good if I do nothing at all

E ven when times are rough I'll push through like I always do

R eaching this goal may be tough but I am me. I am helpful, kind, friendly, a sympathetic person who likes video games so I will work harder and smarter.

Matthew Boyes (11)
Hornchurch High School, Hornchurch

This Is Me

This is me
If you like me or not
I will not change
You will never catch me acting strange
I am integral and brave
I am an extrovert
I will never hide in my cave
I am strong like a lion
I've got support from my family and friends
And most important of all
I've got King Jesus by my side
I am athletic and hard-working
Watch me climb mountains
Just to make my family proud
And soon you will see a massive crowd
Just trying to find me
I've got my dreams all planned and set out
Watch me fly high to get them
I will use the support to get me there faster.

Perry Nkeng (11)
Hornchurch High School, Hornchurch

Myself

My name is Parker-J
This is my poem
I am an excitable, extroverted young man who likes to hit punching bags.

I'm a quarter Irish
I love my family
But they can be very tiring!
I can get very angry at the little things in life
But my friends and family get me through it
Because they are precisely terrific.

I recently got into a football team
This is very special to me
Many people don't know this but I like to play fists with my dad
Not for real obviously!
My family is very proud of me
And I am proud of them.

This has been about me, Parker-J.

Parker-J Harper (11)
Hornchurch High School, Hornchurch

All About Me

A m a big fan of KSI
L ove video games like Fortnite
L ike to collect Pokémon cards

A lways kind and forgiving and ready to help
B rown hair and blue eyes
O verwatch, Fall Guys, Discord, YouTube and WhatsApp are my favourites
U pwards is the only direction to go to improve me
T hankful for my family and friends

R eady for anything trying to get in my way
O verworking to do the best I can
M ale and I was born in Romford
A pples are my favourite fruit
N ever back down and never give up.

Roman Hartley (12)
Hornchurch High School, Hornchurch

I Love Gaming!

Some people think I am a fool for wasting my knowledge on gaming
But the truth is I'm just cool
People call me bad
But the truth is that they are just sad
Because I win and they lose
Sometimes I skip dinner
But that is because I'm trying to be a winner
I don't touch the grass
That's because I'm always catching the bus to my next event
Some people find it hard to lead in a tournament game
But for me it's just a breeze
I play with such ease
This makes my friends unable to breathe
The truth is... if I keep up my game
I will gain some fame.

Abdul Zahir Ali (11)
Hornchurch High School, Hornchurch

This Is Me

This is me
I'm quite creative
I'm also very passionate about dancing
I love all my friends and family
They make me feel happy and positive about everything
I am quite adventurous
I love to travel and see new places
I like meeting new people
I am quite enthusiastic and funny
I love all animals and I love caring for them
I am a very loyal person
I will never share anyone else's secrets
I am quite generous
I think I get that from my mum
She loves making people happy and so do I
I am also Lithuanian
I can speak fluent Lithuanian as well!

Auguste Guzauskaite (12)

Hornchurch High School, Hornchurch

This Is Me

This is me
I can be as outrageous as a bee
Or as calm as the sea
I am as loyal as a dog
I am as fast as a cat
I can be as still as a log
Or as sneaky as a rat
I am as brave as a bear
I am as funny as a clown
So that means I can change your frown
I can be as scary as a beast
So I recommend that sometimes you leave
I love my brown and black hair
I have perfect brown eyes
My perfect brown eyes
Are quite a big size
That's the most about me
As you can see
Now I am going to watch TV
Because that's just me.

Aamani Bains (11)
Hornchurch High School, Hornchurch

I Like Games

It is a good game
But only one can win
Only one can take the trophy
Out there, there is always competition
We will win the trophy
It is so far but so close
I can feel it in my hands
Coming close
But you can't win without a challenge
A challenge beyond the sky
There is always a different level to complete
But in the end we will either fail or win
Taking part is what matters
We've played so many games
It takes hours of hard work and grinding to make it to the top
People may try and stop you but...
Keep going!

Kofi Crontsil (11)
Hornchurch High School, Hornchurch

This Is Me

Identity - what is it?
Everyone's identity is different
So what is yours?
Mine's the army
I've always dreamed of being in the army
Training every day
But this is only a small part of my identity
The rest of it includes
Football, swimming, karate, tennis and so much more
But what makes this my identity?
It's what I love doing
And my goals are related to them
Many more things build up our identity
Pets, your music taste and so much more
Everyone's identity is different
So what is yours?

Isabelle Kersey (12)
Hornchurch High School, Hornchurch

All About Me

Around twelve years ago, a certain child was born
That child was me, I would like to tell you all about me
I am an overall approachable person
Sometimes I'm misunderstood, sometimes I'm in a bad mood
I enjoy playing a game
I hope to be flooded with fame
My pets consist of two cats
One of my fears is rats!
My life goal is to go skydiving
I hope to be driving
I cherish my family
I love the flowers that are known as lily
My sisters are rather silly
I am the oldest child
My hair is very wild.

Alfie Champion (12)
Hornchurch High School, Hornchurch

Try

I am made of kindness, I'm respectful, caring and open-minded.
I like to play music and to draw and read.
I also love to sleep.
When I lose in a competition or I get upset, my friends are there to pick me up and comfort me.
I try to be the best I can.
I don't like to be teased in any way.
I try my best.
I don't care about the rest.
My family supports me when they can.
Even when they are not too good at that.
I sometimes feel horrible because of my anxiety
But in the end I try my best no matter what.

Isabella Terrochaine (13)
Hornchurch High School, Hornchurch

Humayra's Life

Okay, listen up!
Firstly, I really love my family
But the one thing I despise is cheese
Plus my favourite colour is green
My eyes are dark brown
But what I really like is when I turn my frown upside down
I like sleeping in my bed
Playing in the shed
But when Dad comes in I would rather play dead
Look, I'm crazy and rebellious mostly
I'm smart, funny and kind
But if you touch my cat I'll give you a piece of my mind
Okay, this is going to sound corny
But thanks for listening to my story!

Humayra Islam (12)
Hornchurch High School, Hornchurch

Independence

Inside all our hearts we have a soft spot for a special
something
We may try and hide it or deny it
Mine is family
Being around them makes me feel at peace
Their happiness is very important to me
My background plays a significant role
It reminds me that no matter who we are or where we are
from
Anything is achievable if you really want it
A wise person told me that
I try and remember it every day
Be you, nobody can stop that
Not even your family
Your friends
It's all up to you.

Amy Asowata (13)
Hornchurch High School, Hornchurch

This Is Me

This is me, I am kind
I also have a great mind.

I've been told I'm very curious
But I'm also anxious.

I think I'm friendly
But my friends think I'm deadly.

I am very creative but also a drama queen
I'm as sporty as a machine and I'm not that mean.

I'm very clumsy
I am also very clever.

D etermined
E xcellent
N ice
N eat
I ntelligent
E xtravagant

This is me!

Dennie Hardwicke (12)
Hornchurch High School, Hornchurch

This Is Me

This is me
I am in creative mode
This is me
I am in a good mood

I am a curious boy
Not really a mischievous boy
I love dinosaurs
I wear glasses
But I am not a thesaurus

I am a young lad
An infant, a juvenile
Whatever you say
I'm all the same

I follow Islam
Praying every day for my family and everyone
I'm artistic
I pick up a pencil
I make my fantasies on paper

I go by the name of Tarif
Adios, goodbye, ciao!

Tarif Rehan (12)
Hornchurch High School, Hornchurch

This Is Me, This Is My Life

I am Zane,
My life has been good but it has also been rough,
There have been a lot of things that have happened to me,
They have helped me become who I am today,
If not for my hard-working mum and dad
There would have been a lot of things that I would have not
achieved to this day,
Some may think of me as optimistic
Others may think of me as pessimistic
But I think I am an ambitious, determined and confident
individual,
And although I may fail,
I believe that some day I will prevail.

Zane Thompson (11)
Hornchurch High School, Hornchurch

This Is Me

A ccepting you for who you are
M oody, we all have our downside
A nxious, be careful to never hurt anybody
R andom, we all want a bit of excitement
A mazing minds create great things
H appy people influence others to change

D efiant, I take my stand to make things right
U nusual, there is no one like me
F aithful, you can always rely on me
F unny, I will light up a rainbow
Y ou are you and this is me.

Amarah Duffy (11)

Hornchurch High School, Hornchurch

I Am Jeremiah

If you don't know me, I am Jeremiah
I like reading, it makes me feel on fire
First I will tell you I am not a liar
As I'm writing this poem, my IQ is getting higher
Now here are some facts about me
I once got stung by a bee
Every day I make my mum tea
My favourite snack is a chocolate bar
When I grow up I wish to have a car
Speaking about wishes
I wish to have my favourite dishes
Which are lasagne and macaroni
With a sneaky bit of Mum's tea!

Jeremiah Quamina (12)
Hornchurch High School, Hornchurch

This Is Me

Me, myself and I

N ice
I ntelligent
C arefree
H umorous
O rganised
L oving
A dventurous
S entimental

This is me
I can be intelligent
When I think of more creative ways
To do things

This is me
I can be adventurous
And try something new

This is me
I'll be carefree
When I don't care
About others' opinions

This is me.

Nicholas Burghelea (11)
Hornchurch High School, Hornchurch

This Is Me

This is me
I am a steady stream
I like to be right but never normally am
I am as tall as a house
I am as quiet as a mouse

This is me
A talented queen
I believe in myself and live my dreams
One day I will get there
And fulfil the dreams that await me

This is me
As energetic as a rabbit
As annoying as a snake
That can sneak very slowly from a lake

This is me
My heart is compassionate for those who seek love.

Maci Moore (11)
Hornchurch High School, Hornchurch

This Is Me

She's bold and brave and lets nothing get in her way
Not even on a bad day
Such as today
But she has never called 'Mayday'

She's very friendly but can be shy
And nobody knows why
Sometimes she is out of place
But she fixes it at a slow pace

She's very loud
And her family doesn't know how
Even though she's very proud
She's very cool but she can sometimes be a fool
Although she thinks she is cool.

Zara Kasule (11)
Hornchurch High School, Hornchurch

This Is Me

This is me
My name's Alice
I wish I lived in a palace
This is me
Loving and kind
But sometimes when I am stressed I need to unwind
This is me
I like to listen to songs
I have hair that is curly and long
This is me
Very caring but don't make me angry
Or I will be daring
This is me
I am very short
But when I am in school I want to abort
This is me
I have many cats
They sat with me when I studied for my SATs.

Alice Mae Joy (11)
Hornchurch High School, Hornchurch

Stage Fright

Talking, talking, talking
Better than just walking
Talking in front of groups of people
Just makes me think we're not equal

My heartbeat quickens
But my best friend thinks we're chickens
Breathe in, breathe out
Sweat dripping
My heart ripping
People laughing
Makes me feel like I'm dancing

Time to sit back down
Hopefully I don't go with a frown
My heartbeat racing
I don't want to go chasing.

Jannat Kaur (13)
Hornchurch High School, Hornchurch

This Is Me

My name is Sofiia and I'm from Ukraine
I am stressed about my secondary school because I don't
know many things
At my core you will find that I'm really talkative and helpful
I could be a bit rude, angry and mean
If some things are annoying to me
My biggest fears are big dolls, storms and natural disasters
My phobia is claustrophobia
My family, friends, siblings, grandparents and likes
Because I am funny, kind, happy, strong, grateful.

Sofiia Varvarych (11)
Hornchurch High School, Hornchurch

This Is Me

This is me and I am brave
And sometimes my friends call me Dave

People say I have a great imagination
My family say I'm creative
My favourite hobby is drawing
My favourite Harry Potter character is Dobby

I have lots of siblings
They say I am loyal
But sometimes my mum says
I'm as annoying as a boil

I am funny but also a dummy
Everyone can agree
I hope you liked my poem
As this is all about me!

Jaimee Hardwicke (12)
Hornchurch High School, Hornchurch

No One Is Perfect

Some people think everyone is perfect
they think that living in a mansion
being famous
having loads of money
is important
but most of the time that's not how it really is.
I am a thirteen-year-old girl
I have four brothers and two sisters
I live with my dad, stepmum and stepsister
some people would consider me and my life as perfect but it's not.
Remember: people know your name, not your story.
No one is perfect.

Sadie Brewer (13)
Hornchurch High School, Hornchurch

This Is Me

I am Samuel,
I am a fierce warrior,
I'll try my best
But it might not be the best.

I am smart,
I am brave,
I will not give up,
Until I am in my grave.

Sometimes I'm stressed,
But I always try my best,
Although I may fail
I believe that I will always prevail.

I am strong courageous and brave,
I am made up of fame,
Some day I will win
And be an inspiration to the world.

Samuel Olaru (11)
Hornchurch High School, Hornchurch

This Is Me

An ambitious boy
With hopes and dreams
Filled with joy
This is me!

The pillars that do
Hold me up
I am Hindu
This is who I am

Sometimes I find
Collapsed are my walls
Anger seeps through
While darkness spreads

However, with the light
That's my family
Everything changes
To again be bright

With my close ones
That helped me see
Who I am
This is me!

Rahul Gunputh (11)
Hornchurch High School, Hornchurch

Family Is My Life

F avourite place to be is with them, wherever they are, that is my home

A ttached to them for life, something you can't escape

M ixing up the twins on a daily basis and playing tricks which everyone loves

I will always love them despite the constant arguments and fights

L ook out for each other at all times, defend them in public but teach them in private

Y earn for adoration and care, this is my family.

Anna Vimal (13)
Hornchurch High School, Hornchurch

This Is Me

This is me, I like art
To top it off, I'm as fast as a dart
Sports is my thing
However, I don't like to sing.

People say I'm nice
But it comes at a price
I love Hobbycraft
But I try not to be daft.

Now I am in Hornchurch High
It's quite nice
Now I'm settled in
I try not to throw my homework in the bin.

I've enjoyed writing this poem
But now I have to be going!

Sienna Bird (11)
Hornchurch High School, Hornchurch

All About Me

At my core you will find that
I am as confident as a new president giving a speech in
front of a massive country
I am as courageous as a soldier risking his life for his own
country
I am as anxious as a refugee fleeing their country, not
knowing if they will make it
I am as loyal to my religion as a martyr who was tortured to
death
I am as afraid as a little kid in the middle of a war
I am as heartbroken as a parent losing their child.

Musa Ahmed (12)
Hornchurch High School, Hornchurch

This Is Me!

Every day people are so kind to me
Like my family, friends and everyone
It must be my personality: funny, kind, stubborn and honest
I like maths, history and art
I want to be an accountant in the future
Due to my intelligence and creativity
Some of my fears are spiders and snakes and many more
creepy-crawlies
My favourite foods are pancakes, pizza, seafood and
lasagne
I try my best to be the best person I can possibly be.

Lewis Hallel (12)

Hornchurch High School, Hornchurch

I Am The Brightest Star In The Sky

I am the brightest star in the sky
Even though I am a bit shy
I dig many things from my book
But I am a bad cook
Everyone says I am very mad today
But I know that I am the brightest star in the sky
I am scared of many things around me
But the sounds of animals like a dog and cat distract me
Everyone around me says I want to do that and I want to do this
But I don't care because I am the mayor of all stars.

Amala Maria Baiju (12)
Hornchurch High School, Hornchurch

This Is Me

D oesn't give up - always try my best in everything I do

U nderstanding - always listens and helps people

S taying positive - always trying my best and trying again if something goes wrong

T rying to go for my dreams, trying to become a footballer or an athlete

I ntelligent - likes maths and is good at it and grammar

N ever stops trying - stays hard-working and never backs down or gives up.

Dustin Ramirez-Vera (11)
Hornchurch High School, Hornchurch

This Is Me

This is me
I am kind
I am the kindest person you can find

I am a secretive person without a doubt
I am quite the introvert yet I like to go out
I have a strong love for animals, you could say they love me
If I had a dog I would go on a walk and sit under a tree

I have an uncle called Tony
We are both very lonely
I often listen to music in my room
Sometimes I feel like dancing with a broom.

Melissa Marshall (11)
Hornchurch High School, Hornchurch

This Is Grace

I am Grace
I love animals
My dog is my best friend
She gives the best cuddles
She always licks my face
I enjoy history
My favourite topic is World War II
My best friend is the kindest
She is always there for me during my highs and lows
My mum is the best
She can beat me in any test
She is very funny and helps me
She deserves the world
My dad is kind
He does his best all the time.

Grace Gibbons (12)
Hornchurch High School, Hornchurch

This Is Me

These are the bricks that built me
My family take care of me
My name is Sephora
And this is me
I love to take care of my family
My life is amazing because of the people that are in it
I'm loving and caring
'Cause of my family
Let's be honest
Loud and proud because it runs in my genes
I'm Christian and Congolese
My mum is proud of me
'Cause I'm bright and honest.

Sephora Nsongo (12)
Hornchurch High School, Hornchurch

Embracing Me

I am proud of who I am
What you think of me
I don't give a damn

I am confident like a roaring lion
Fearlessly embracing my unique pride
I am strong and brave, even if I may have lied

My family is my strength, a bond unbreakable
I have friends who love me
That's enough for me

I am who I am and I will never change
So keep your judgement to yourself or else.

Dolcie Powell Bryan (13)
Hornchurch High School, Hornchurch

This Is Me

I am John
I come from the Philipines
I am eleven
I am playful, funny and smart
My height is average
My religion is Christianity
I like biking and playing with my friends
I am grateful for my talents from my grandparents
On my dad's side of the family, my grandmother is a bowling champion
She won at least eight trophies
My grandpa is a famous musician and he is the lead singer.

John Erdozo (11)
Hornchurch High School, Hornchurch

Unique

I have many flaws I admit
But I realise no one's perfect
Even when I fail I stay resilient
I'm an extrovert I have to say
I try and make new friends every day.

Many people have misconceptions about me
It still doesn't stop me from being happy
People say your mistakes define you
And maybe it's true
No matter what they say
Everyone is unique in their own way.

Kaitlin Ciobotaru (11)
Hornchurch High School, Hornchurch

As The Sky Goes By...

As the sky goes by
Our time goes by
Holding pain and sadness

Never having someone to support you through your misery
Your safe space is your only hope
The ache of every day makes you even more sensitive

The cries and tears are not worth your time
Tears dripping like a hopeless lime

As the sky goes by
All you want to do is hide
As you hear all those lies.

Nandika Sharma (13)
Hornchurch High School, Hornchurch

Life In My Shoes

F rom Dagenham, I love football and support West Ham

R oblox fan, I like to use computers

E ssex is the county I am from, it is my home

D oes not like school, it is like a prison!

D oes lots of sports, likes rap music

I am strong but when people are rude to me I am very sensitive

E xtremely fast at running but I lose my breath very quickly.

Freddie Debruin (11)

Hornchurch High School, Hornchurch

This Is Me

I like listening to music
I like to play badminton
My career is important to me the most
I am from India
I am a Hindu
I believe in more than one god
My name means being brave and confident
There is a freedom fighter within my name
There is a movie with my name
I like doing maths equations
I like to be around people
I like to do classical dances.

Manikarnika Rai (13)
Hornchurch High School, Hornchurch

This Is Me

This is me
I am more talented than you think
I am as precious as a diamond ring
Everyone becomes emotive when I am creative
A great daughter I am to my father
I want to become a doctor
I have a beautiful life
A beautiful family I have
A peaceful life
What a wonderful Earth we live on
I am as busy as a bee
I feel enthusiastic when I see the sea.

Alarmelu Aiswarya Periyakaruppan (12)
Hornchurch High School, Hornchurch

This Is Me

This is me...
I am loud but I am also quiet
I might express myself and sing or I will keep to myself
I might get good grades or I might need extra help
I am loyal and I will always be there for you if you need
someone
It is okay not to know what your qualities are
As long as you don't change for someone else
I might not be like you but I am happy being myself.

Niamh Spindler (12)
Hornchurch High School, Hornchurch

This Is Me

M astermind, I'm pretty smart
A thletic, I love loads of sports
T hankful for my life and my family
T ireless, I have a lot of energy

D auntless, I'm brave
I ntelligent, I'm good at maths
X mas is my favourite holiday
E ating, I love eating pizza
Y oung, I'm only twelve.

Matt Dixey (12)
Hornchurch High School, Hornchurch

Stop Racism

It's funny how people bully people
With their colour, size and where they are from
Peers, why can we not stop bullying?
It's such a bad thing to do to people
Don't we know that it might hurt people's feelings?
It's awful to see how people abuse each other over their colour, weight and height
Let's stop racism and bullying together!

Sururah Ilelaboye (11)

Hornchurch High School, Hornchurch

This Is Me

I am like a diamond in the sky
Even though I am too shy to go on stage because of making
a wrong move
I am as brave as a lion
I am as fast as a cheetah
I love playing football
So I can exercise to get my body into the right shape
I eat vegetables to stay healthy
So I don't put on excess weight
This is me, Bryan.
Aiming to be the best.

Bryan Aikpitanyi (12)
Hornchurch High School, Hornchurch

This Is Me

My name is Lacey
I like to lie
I don't know why
I don't like sports
I don't really know why
I like basketball
But not baseball
I like watching football
But I don't like playing it
I go to Hornchurch High
But I need to learn how to do a tie
I like playing with my friends
I like talking to them.

Lacey Butler (11)
Hornchurch High School, Hornchurch

This Is Me

H igher than the clouds
O ver the seas
L aughing along with my family
L ooking down below
I 'm waving hello
E xcited by what I'm going to see...

M aybe I'm wondering what it's going to be
A drenaline running through my body
Y ou might want to join me.

Hollie-May Scott (13)
Hornchurch High School, Hornchurch

This Is Me

The world is small and so am I
Look it in the eye
And you will see creativity shining through me
My world is vast
Full of colours
That will forever last
And every flick of my brush
I am painting my confidence

I am as bright as a shining star
Rising, rising, rising
For I am me and no one else
That is me.

Rehnuma Tajrin (11)
Hornchurch High School, Hornchurch

This Is Me - I Am Kaan

This is me
I am Kaan
I'm not going to say anymore
Let's get on with the poem

I am kind
I am also quite funny
I am the kindest person you'll find
Most of the time I'm happy

Sometimes I can be introverted
Sometimes I can be extroverted
I like to game
Hopefully I will rise to fame.

Kaan Isikgun (11)
Hornchurch High School, Hornchurch

Save Me

Save me from the future
it's too close to me
doing the same thing every day
my childhood wasted away
take me back
so many things I want to see
want to do
stuck in a time loop
take me away
take me back to the old days
'cause I'm afraid
want to be little me
with no worries
please save me.

Archie Wyatt (13)
Hornchurch High School, Hornchurch

I Am Me

I am
Rainforests and sunsets
I like long walks
And quiet times
I value honesty, humour and peace of mind
I can be fearsome when my ideas are challenged
But I thrive on intelligent conversations
I love Earth and all its animals
I can be counted on to help
I have strong feelings when life is threatened
This is me.

Naya Garcia Clegg (11)
Hornchurch High School, Hornchurch

Who Am I?

I am me, not anyone else, me
I fly three flags - Jamaica, Ghana, England
Red, gold, black, green
Blue, white - as seen
On the flags of these great countries
I am bold, strong, resilient, productive and fearless
Who am I?
Mixed some say
But I am proud
I am brave
I am seen as a maze
Waiting to be solved.

Esi Amoa-Sakyi (13)
Hornchurch High School, Hornchurch

This Is Me

This is me, I am as illusive as the sea
As obedient as a dog
As strong as the wind
And as loving as a cat

Shy as a leaf
Dreamy as a cloud
As white as snow
And as sincere as a melody

As unique as a four-leaf clover
As curly as noodles
As resistant as a bear
And as bright as the sun.

Daria-Gabriela Hululei (11)
Hornchurch High School, Hornchurch

I Am Me

I am smart
I like art
We need to know what things are
I am nice
No more knives
I eat food
So do you
I am as brave as a lion
Staring is my favourite thing
But we need to know what to do
We all try to rest
Now let's do our best
I am the brightest star in the sky
Even though I am shy.

Ibrahim Yusuf (12)
Hornchurch High School, Hornchurch

This Is Me

My name is Ava Munday
I love acting
I want to be an actress
That is my dream
I have the best skills you have ever seen
I go to acting classes every Monday after school
If you ever need advice just give me a call
My confidence has grown
I have come very far
When I am older
I hope to be a star.

Ava Munday (11)
Hornchurch High School, Hornchurch

Ocean Child

O ctober and autumn are always going to be the best

C harle the Labrador was always there when I came home

E ngland is where I live but there will always be a special place for Lithuania

A yla will always be my best friend, as long as I live

N athan will always be my special little brother.

Juliette Jogaila (12)

Hornchurch High School, Hornchurch

Autism

A utism is not a disability, it's a superpower
U s - me and you are not the same
T he world is seen differently by me and you
I am always hyperactive and never focused
S ome people think I'm weird but others think I am cool
M y thoughts and feelings are hard to explain.

Freddie Jones (13)
Hornchurch High School, Hornchurch

This Is Me: I Am

This is me, I am supportive
I am sporty, I am energetic

The time is running fast
But it is hard to catch up

I am grateful and loyal
And happy for the friendships I have

I am young and hard-working
I am kind and helpful

I love food
So maybe we can cook sometime.

Nicole Nykante (12)
Hornchurch High School, Hornchurch

This Is Me

I am a girl
I love dogs
I love studying
It is fun
We have fun learning
But sometimes it is kind of boring
In the meantime
When we go home
We do our homework
And then we watch things on our phones
School is fun
We have lots of fun
And they teach us
So much.

Izabela Pultinza (11)
Hornchurch High School, Hornchurch

This Is Me!

This is me and my name is Ronnie
Some of my friends call me Donny
I love West Ham but I don't like ham
I'm quite a picky eater
And in the winter I need a heater

In school I wish my handwriting was neater
I go to Hornchurch High
At school I had to learn how to do a tie.

Ronnie Holloway (11)
Hornchurch High School, Hornchurch

This Is Me

People judge, people make assumptions
But that's not who you are
That's not who I am
I am brave
I am kind
I am fearless
And no one can take that away from me
Who I am is who I am
Not who you are
We are all different and that's what will never change.

Kayla Cooper (11)
Hornchurch High School, Hornchurch

Visiting My Home Country

I am a brown girl who lives far away from her blood country
The problem is learning my home language is hard so I don't even try
Elderly people have a laugh when they hear my accent
They test me on my English
When I visit my home country
Fleeing from it would be a huge wish.

Mehek Bhuiyan (11)
Hornchurch High School, Hornchurch

This Is Me

C aring to others
H elpful to peers
A dmirable to youngsters
R eliable when needed
L oving to my family
O utgoing with my friends
T eamwork makes the dream work
T imid with new people
E ffective to work with.

Charlotte Miles (14)

Hornchurch High School, Hornchurch

This Is Me

G reat as can be, this is me
R eady to start, this is my part
A mazing things I complete, this is the best part of me
C ousins and family are important to me
I am happy because of my family
E mbracing myself is the best I can do.

Gracie Bennett (12)
Hornchurch High School, Hornchurch

Running From Reality

R unning from reality
E scaping past infinity
A ll the way to Jupiter
L onging to not be stupider
I nto another dimension
T o create a new sensation
Y awning my way through a new way of communication.

Robert Dunas (11)
Hornchurch High School, Hornchurch

Autumn

The days get shorter
And the nights get longer
It's just autumn

The leaves fall
Dancing down like they are at a ball
It's just autumn

Orange leaves blooming through
It gives everybody a clue
It's autumn.

Chloe Butler (13)
Hornchurch High School, Hornchurch

Honesty

This is me
A somebody
A person who lives not entirely free
Though no one is trapped and neither am I
I am still bored within this great sky
You see
I have to get good grades
I have to be smart
I have to have grand prospects!

Divine Apinoko (13)
Hornchurch High School, Hornchurch

This Is Me

This is me
I'm as smart as an owl
Or a lion on the prowl
As sweet as sugar, as cool as a tree
And as weary as the sea
I'm as cold as ice
And everything nice
I'm as slick as mice
And as kind as life.

Spencer Wheeler (11)
Hornchurch High School, Hornchurch

All About Me

A big fan of seafood
L ikes to listen to music
I maginative and creative
Z ones out a lot of the time
A big lover of cats and cute animals
H ates the subjects maths and Spanish.

Alizah Islam (12)
Hornchurch High School, Hornchurch

This Is Me

This is me
I'm resilient
Most people think I'm brilliant
I am kind
I also have a great mind
I have short hair
I am not scared of a bear
I like summer 'cause it's hot
I like KFC a lot.

Alex Buterchi (12)
Hornchurch High School, Hornchurch

The Only Thing I Need

I may not be the most athletic
I'm definitely not the best at sport
But I have my horse
I love my sport
That feeling when my breath starts to slow
Everything stops
My adrenaline runs.

Ryann Rookard (14)
Hornchurch High School, Hornchurch

This Is Me

At my core you will find
A warm-hearted place
Filled with much glee and grace
So if you are in the spot
Just know you mean a lot.

Tyler Allen (14)
Hornchurch High School, Hornchurch

My Past Life

Today, I had a flashback of my past life,
I only just moved into my new house.
It was such a nice house and it had a pretty big garden -
so, we decided to get dogs.
We got three dogs.
I got one,
my brother got one,
and there was a family dog.
My brother and I shared a bathroom and
my little brother was a baby then
so stayed with my parents.
It was my birthday
and it was the best birthday
of my life.
I got a quad and clothes and lots of other stuff including a
BMX bike.
One day, it was the worst day of my life -
we had to sell my dogs and had to move house again.
The day we moved house,
I went to my friend's house
and then it was the big reveal... The new house!
I had a big bedroom and, this time, I didn't have to share;
my brother had his own bedroom downstairs -
it used to be the dining room.

John-James Read (11)
Hylands School, Chelmsford

My Animals

In my garden, with dewdrop grass,
run my little duckies, slapping and quacking with all their friends.
When a pigeon lands, they run up to it with a great big smile
and laugh when it flies away.
Clucking and pecking all day long,
roam my chickens with a pep in their step
and proudly wearing their combs like a crown.
But, just standing there, doing nothing at all
are my bobble-headed chickens.
Pecking at treats and missing them completely,
not a thing going on in their pea-sized brains.
Sniffing and digging are my naughty rabbits,
escaping and trying to get into the house,
begging for more and more treats.
Munching on carrots until their bellies are full to sunbathing in the sun
are their favourite things to do.

Persephonie Searson (12)
Hylands School, Chelmsford

A Bit About Me

As elegant white swans calmly glide through the lake,
relaxing swooshing sounds are the sounds the seas make.
Just like me, they can easily get angry, but are also chill
not weak, but get ill.
I know it sounds mean
however, I am as strong as a hawk and that is key
another outstanding thing
is I am a lion from within.
I love acting, drawing and my family
these are things with a meaning to me.
So, I may not be perfect, but I am not that bad, sometimes I
am low-spirited
but I won't give up until I win this.
I have a lot on my chest
and I am not the best
but this is me
and that is the best I can be.

Ivy-Sola Gaci (11)
Hylands School, Chelmsford

This Is Me

My luscious brown eyes get lots of compliments
from people who write documents.
My perfect personality is so perfect I couldn't ask for
anything else.

Football, football is so fun
my family members love to run.
Wink, wink,
I love to think
Lucozade is my favourite drink.

Teeth so clean
it's a dream
sleep, sleep is the best
when it's time for some rest.
Let your mind unwind
and your best imagination you will find
sunrise, sunshine
Taurus is my star sign.

Albie Lodge (11)
Hylands School, Chelmsford

My Lovely Lady

Biscuit is a lovely lady and she is also crazy,
when I take her for a walk, she is very lazy.
She makes a grey day sunny,
when she is funny,
my little brother loves her,
and her beautiful fur,
when I feed her, she is excited
and also very delighted,
but when I walk away,
she barks all day,
when I march back, she smiles in my face.
When I'm down, she lights me back up,
when she smiles, she makes me want to love.

Tommy-Alfie Read (12)
Hylands School, Chelmsford

BFG Kid

I am laidback
Like a recliner chair
But also lively and active

I am competitive
With any sport
If I like the sport
I will buy the kit and practise
Practise, practise
I become single-minded
To the exclusion of everything else
Until I get bored with it.

I am not just observant
I have 20/20 vision
With my hazel eyes
Which are piercing but warm.

I am as tall as a lamppost
But I don't like heights
My elastic, stretchy legs
Reach far and wide
Helped by my BFG conditioner.

I like maths and English
But dislike courgettes and celery

I have an excessive love of fruit
Especially apples and oranges
Passionfruit is my favourite, though
And I could eat the whole world's supply.

I want to be a builder
It's a family tradition
And it's good pay too
But my dream is to not need a job .
Although I am a leader and also loyal.

I have an odd sense of humour
But it makes me entertaining
I am the class joker
But I also moan a lot.

C ompetitive
A micable
L ively
L aidback
U naffected
M iserable.

Callum Wilson (13)
Millgate School, Leicester

This Is Me

Disturbingly, I made noises in the back.
I didn't want to wait until break time to play football.
I wanted to be the best
And to dominate everyone who played football.
I am very competitive.
I don't want to lose any match.
I love to read and game
But I also love playing games
With my family.

F iery
I ntelligent
N ice
L ively
E nergetic
Y appy

P layful
E nthusiastic
N oisy
F ast
O utstanding
L aughable
D opey.

Finley Penfold (13)
Millgate School, Leicester

All About Me

I am as talkative as birds on a summer morning
But also sort of an introverted person.
I can be arrogant but also warm-hearted
To the people I know.
In my spare time, I game
To escape reality.
My fear is really fast roller coasters
However, a straight drop gives me
An adrenaline rush.
My dream is to become a chef
Because I'm quite good in my food lessons.
I have a lot of love for my family
However, I fall out with my brother
I have a few positive things to say about myself
But my family and friends say kind things about me.

Zaak Bate
Millgate School, Leicester

Me

C omical
O bsessive
B ubbly
Y appy

N eedy
E nergetic
W arm-hearted
C aring
O bservant
M oany
B rave

I have an infectious laugh
Everyone laughs when I do.
I do not like my dimples,
But Chelsea likes them very much.
I am very observant.
I love watching the world go by.
I love gaming and cars
And know lots about them.
I am funny but can be annoying,
Some call me the class clown.

Coby Newcomb (13)
Millgate School, Leicester

Funny

I am funny but can be annoying
I'm autistic but 'normal'
I like chilling, but I also like going out
I'm really lazy but also really hyper
I'd like a pet monkey, but I dislike spiders
I'm really creative but also adventurous
I have loads of friends, but I only speak to some of them
Don't forget, I am funny but can be annoying.

Riegan Douglas (15)
Millgate School, Leicester

My Life

My hair rising in the wind
Waking up to another day of 'paradise'
The annoying people think
I annoy them,
But I don't.
Taming the animal in the game,
I can't wait until I go home
The day of the competition is on.
I flip into the day.
I flip like a pancake
Because I am a pancake
I flip every second
Every day.

Henry Ind (15)
Millgate School, Leicester

This Is Me, Harvey

H appy
A ctive
R ogue
V erbal
E xcited
Y oung

T ired
A ngry
Y oung
L oud
O rganised
R ude

F ootballer
O rderly
S illy
T idy
E ager
R ugged.

Harvey Taylor Foster (13)

Millgate School, Leicester

Raven's Quavers

Eyes as twinkling as an amber stone
Hair as wavy as an ocean
And as bushy as a grizzly bear
Clothes so baggy as I'm only 5ft 1
Weird but lovely
Shy at first but loud after...

R espectful
A dmirable
V ibrant
E nthusiastic
N eat?

Raven Whitworth (13)
Millgate School, Leicester

Fifteen-Year-Old

Fifteen years old
Brown-haired and brown-eyed boy
Footballer and video gamer
Kind and caring
Loves sisters, brother and Mum
Highly ambitious
Wants to be successful
Wants a good job when older
Would like a friend who is:
Funny and caring.

Declan Mark Kean (15)
Millgate School, Leicester

This Is Me, Alex McCarthy

A rtistic.

L oyal.

E nergetic.

X enomorph.

M odest.

C aring.

C razy.

A mazing.

R ealistic.

T ruthful.

H appy.

Y oung.

Alex McCarthy (13)

Millgate School, Leicester

This Is Me, Mason

M essy
A nnoying
S porty
O utrageous
N ice

R ude
U nderstanding
S elf-confident
S illy
E xcitable
L azy
L ove.

Mason Russell (13)
Millgate School, Leicester

This Is Me. Daisy

D angerous
A ctive
I rresponsible
S assy
Y ummy

C osy
H yper
A rtistic
P retty
M oody
A nnoying
N ice.

Daisy Chapman (13)
Millgate School, Leicester

This Is Me, Matilda!

M essy
A ngry
T ired
I ntelligent
L oud
D angerous
A ctive

C lever
O riginal
L oved
E legant
Y oung.

Matilda Coley (13)
Millgate School, Leicester

This Is Me, Liam

L ovely Liam
I ntelligent
A mazing
M otivated

K ind
I ncredible
R hythmic
K nowledgeable.

Liam Kirk (14)
Millgate School, Leicester

This Is Me, Simon

Brother
Confident, creative
Caring, supportive, musical
Passionate, proud, trustworthy, loyal
Enthusiastic, sporty, annoying
Loving, happy
Friendly.

Simon Ely (14)
Millgate School, Leicester

This Is Me! Codey!

Uncle
Loyal, lovely
Basketballer, cook, artistic
Active, supportive, friendly, kind
Happy, helpful, homely,
Petrolhead, practical,
Son.

Codey Wright-Prime (15)
Millgate School, Leicester

This Is Me

My long, silky, brown hair
Ocean-blue eyes
Happy smile
My bad attitude
Caring about people
Attempting to make funny jokes.

Carson Birch (15)
Millgate School, Leicester

Oliver!

O bnoxious
L iverpool fan
I deal
V aluable
E nergetic
R esilient.

Oliver Newitt (13)

Millgate School, Leicester

Me!

K nowledgeable
A rticulate
Y oung
D azzling
O ptimistic
N ice.

Kaydon Jones (13)
Millgate School, Leicester

I Am Me

In a world where dreams can take their flight
A young black girl, her future shining bright
At just the age of two, a burn did brand,
Her right hand's courage, her strengths steadfast stand

Through life's journey, she faced the bitter breeze
Racism's whispers like rustling leaves in trees
Xenophobia's shadow tried to dim her way,
But she found the strength to brighten every day
She ventured from distant shores to the UK's embrace
A land where they can find their right place

With aspiration soaring, her heart takes flight,
She yearns to be a pilot, to reach the highest height
With each challenge she encountered, she's grown strong,
In her heart, resilience dances like a song
She's the young black girl, a beacon in the sky
Gazing at the stars, determined to touch the high.
Though her right hand bears a mark of the past
It's a symbol of the strength that's sure to last.
She'll take to the skies, spread her wings and scar
A pilot, a dreamer, forever wanting more
In the face of adversity, she stands tall and bold

A story of courage and dreams yet untold
This young black girl, at thirteen, sets her aim
To conquer the heavens, to rise in her own name

Her right hand held high as her story unfolds, with every
step she carries her heritage, her song
Where she'd grow strong
With each challenge faced, she'll continue to stand
A symbol of strength in this diverse, united land.

Elaine Nyashanu (13)
Norton College, Norton

The Colour Blue

I love the colour blue, don't you?
The colour of the sky and the sea
That I'd happily think about all day and all week.
I love the colour blue, don't you?
Azure, ocean or simply just blue.

But what if others didn't like it as much as me or you,
What if they decided to cancel the colour blue?
Would that make you sad? Me too,
But the colour of sadness would be erased alongside blue

The world would continue unaffected
Sky and sea known just as them
No need to place a colour alongside
Because in a rainbow blue could be faded to hide.

I suppose it's not an important colour,
Such as green for grass
Or yellow for sun
Because without them the order would be none.

How would orange fade to green
If green didn't exist and yellow wasn't there to link them
But blue could simply fade and be forgotten
Creating no problems?

Sometimes, I feel like the colour blue
Stood in the middle of the room, unseen
Because there's someone there slightly better than me
I know it's only my expectations I'm not meeting
I make everyone else proud
And that makes me so happy.

But still I strive for perfection.
I thrive in it.

So, yes,
Sometimes, I feel like the colour blue,
But be honest, don't you?

Emily Umpleby (13)
Norton College, Norton

Girls Grow Up

I am a teenage girl.
I sing in the shower,
And light candles at night.
I like wearing jewellery,
And listening to music in the morning.
I am a teenage girl.
I burn my waves straight to feel prettier,
And refuse food to feel skinnier.
I curl my eyelashes till my eyes water,
Because that's what boys like, right?
I am a teenage girl.
I try to read books,
Before I go to sleep,
And cling onto the last hope of being 'smart',
Because I used to be good for my age.
But I am a teenage girl now,
And nothing is ever good enough,
Pretty isn't pretty enough
Skinny isn't skinny enough,
And I can never be right.
I am a teenage girl,
But I won't be forever.
One day, I'll miss lipgloss,
And singing in the shower.

I'll long for the time to read,
And the smell of cinnamon candles.
But I'll have grown up.
I won't dress for boys anymore,
Or hate the reflection in the mirror,
I'll embrace my waves,
And droopy eyelashes,
I am a teenage girl.
But, one day, I'll grow up.

Lottie Johnson (13)
Norton College, Norton

Washed Away

Breathe in, breathe out, this is where I want to be,
Feel the sand on my skin, let myself feel free,
Just zone out now, you've done it before,
Listen to the waves, hear how they crash on the shore,

Drifting away, so easy, yet so strangely hard,
If I put too much effort in, I will just feel jarred,
I hear them getting closer, I feel them, I know,
The water, it's coming, it's now my time to show,

The ocean washes over me like a mellow melody,
Conveying it into my piece continues endlessly,
Subtle tension in my bow, it makes me feel complete,
My finger placements on the strings take place in a heartbeat,

Here comes a crescendo, the waves tower above my head,
Let the weight leave my arm, be in my bow instead,
Now the waves will fear me, and I can bear the storm,
Let my music fuel me, and make me feel warm,

All there is that's left to do is make the final straight,
Just a scale from low to high, I know it'll feel great,
As my resplendent song is nearly at its close,
I slip up on just one note, and my tranquillity goes.

Albert Stokes (13)

Norton College, Norton

Shoes

I wish life was like a pair of shoes
once they no longer fit you,
you move on.
I cling to my scruffy Converse,
regardless of the increasing hole that expands the more I
wear them.
Yet my pristine Mary Janes I got last Christmas linger,
patiently waiting to be worn

I wish life was like a pair of shoes
however, sometimes, I don't feel like moving on
sometimes, my old pair suits me better than the new pair
sometimes, I'll force my foot into that old pair and forever
argue that they're comfortable,
no matter the excruciatingly painful blisters I receive
it's fine! Some time and a plaster will do the trick,

I wish life was as simple as changing your shoes,
change is inevitable, we evolve with the rest.
One day, you'll change your shoes and eventually encounter
the perfect pair.
Blisters heal with time, right?
A plaster won't heal scars,
but acceptance can prevent them.

Julia Piechowiak (13)
Norton College, Norton

Kacie Is Me, OK

K icking a football does not entertain me, but Catchphrase is always funny.

A utism and dyspraxia explain me a lot, like making stories that include a plot.

C ats and dogs' arguments can be anywhere, I like cats despite all their hair.

I believe games help with mental health, yet money helps you with your wealth

E ntering social rooms put me at unease, so being alone is not a disease

I nsects, spiders and needles are my fear, from big to small and hidden to clear.

S cience, English and drama, some lessons I like that I think have no karma.

M any songs I like are around the same, made by Lady Gaga or based on a game

E xit the word to go in my own mind, there where no one else can be kind

O range juice and cinnamon buns taste good, better than potatoes ever could

K nowledge helps me with everything, but a small start is a thing.

Kacie Marshall (13)

Norton College, Norton

Be Yourself

It doesn't matter what is on the outside
it matters what is in the inside.

Don't quit.
Suffer now and live the rest of your life a champion.
Success belongs only to those who are willing to work
harder than anyone else.
Never say never because limits, like fears, are often just
illusions

gold medals aren't really made of gold
they're made of blood, sweat, determination and a hard-to-
find alloy called guts.

If you do not believe you can do it
then you have no changes at all.

You have to expect things of yourself
before you can do them

success isn't given.
It's earned on the track
on the field,
in the gym.
With blood, sweat and the occasional tear.

Cadence Joyce-Smith (11) & Naomi Tomasi
Norton College, Norton

And That's Me

With long, blonde hair,
and eyes so blue,
behind my glasses,
my character shines through

I am a true fighter,
brave and bold,
with a heart that's been through stories untold,
at just six months old,
I faced a fight,
with open heart surgery
I have shone so bright.

Dancing is my passion,
it's true,
competitions I've danced through,
with every tap and leap,
I feel alive,
the stage is where I truly thrive.

Hanging out with my best friends,
that's where I belong,
laughing, talking, making memories
all day long

on stage, I will dance and sing,
as a SCBU nurse, the comfort I will bring,
or as an animal carer,
I'll help creatures big and small
during winter, summer, spring and fall.

And that's me, Jessica Thomas.

Jessica Thomas (12)
Norton College, Norton

All Of Me Expressed In A Poem

School starts again, new year, new me.
A few things have changed over the past six weeks.
I like watching films, spending time with my friends, biology,
rain and art.
These are some things I love with all of my heart.
I could add many more to that handy list,
but what I need is biology to help me be a cetologist
In my spare time, I swim, ride horses and draw
I have also started doing quite a bit more.
I would describe myself as creative, short and friendly.
I also wouldn't want to harm someone intentionally.
I would never want to get in a fight
because both of my parents have raised me right.
My family has helped me through all of my stress.
They have also helped me achieve success.

Molly Sterriker (12)
Norton College, Norton

Happy Splashes

Waves, wind, water; water, wind and waves,
As I glide across the shimmering glass-like lake,
Troubles leave and go to their graves,
My mind is focused - I am awake,
Oh, a humid summer's day, I think I might bake.

The main sail blowing in the wind and flying across the sea,
High on life, as they say,
Nothing is getting in my way,
Speeding across the ocean-seeming body of water,
My sailing is my strength as I steer across the bay,
Worries, negativity and fear blow away.

Sailing washes my anxiety off,
It washes away my fear of...
If I have a scary hobby,
Don't make fun of me because it is funny.

Erin Cotton (12)
Norton College, Norton

Me

I don't like to wake up early
School starts at 45, I need to leave by 30
I haven't done my homework
I hope my teacher shows mercy

I'm not a golden girl
I'm a precious pearl
I much prefer to dance and twirl

When the music begins to play
I love to seize the day
I love the notes to take me away
Because dance is my way!

Sylvie Hill (12)
Norton College, Norton

Be Yourself

Don't pretend, make a friend,
they will help you till the end,
don't spoil,
be loyal,
believe in yourself, it isn't hard,
maybe just make a card,
I knew you could do it through and through
I couldn't be anywhere without you.
Believe in yourself, take pride in your work
you're beautiful like this caring Earth!

Cadence Joyce-Smith (11)
Norton College, Norton